Talha Tales

Portugal's Ancient Answer to Amphora Wines

Paul James White

Table of Contents

Acknowledgements   4
How to read this book   5
PART I: FOR THE OENOPHILE   7
Gato's Last Tasca   8
Talha: A Perfect Winemaking Machine   10
Talha's Resurrection   13
Then vs Now   26
To Pés or not to Pés…   28
Talha at the Center of Village Life   34
Talha's Traditional Grape Varieties   37
Potted History, Then and Now   48
Jupiter's Lift Off   57
A New Concept of Terroir & Grand Cru   60
Final Thoughts on Beautiful Pots   61
PART 2: THE PRODUCERS   64
ACV   65
Cooperativa Adega de Borba   68
Cortes de Cima   71
Herdade do Esporão   74
Fitapreta   77
Gerações da Talha   81
Honrado & Pais das Uvas   84
Jose de Sousa   89
Adega Marel   97
Herdade dos Outeiros Altos   102
Quinta da Pigarça & Adega do Canena   105
Casa Relvas   110
Herdade do Rocim   113
Rui Reguinga and Terrenus   122
Susana Esteban   126
Adega Cooperativa Vidigueira, Cuba and Alvito   130
XXVI Talhas   135
PART 3: FOR THE WINE TOURIST   140
A Brief History of Alentejo   141
Visiting the Alentejo   145
Visiting the Regions   147
Eating in Alentejo   155
For the Virtual Tourist   157
Biographies   161
Bibliographic References   163
Glossary of Terms   164
The End   165

Acknowledgements

Firstly, an undying thanks to my rock-solid, pilgrim partner, Jenny Mortimer, who produced this book, in addition to my web page, www.winedisclosures.com. An author in her own right, she also wrote a snazzy little bit on wine tourism tagged onto the end of the book. Not forgetting my two daughters for putting up with my endless irascibility, Chloe Smith, whose impressive palate has managed to savor a few *talha* wines in her time, and my other non-imbibing daughter, Ella White, an eagle-eyed editor and scholar in her own right. I couldn't do without them.

A personal thanks to Jose de Sousa's guiding light, Domingos Soares Franco, Maria Amélia Vaz da Silva and Herdade do Rocim's dynamic duo, Pedro Ribeiro and Catarina Vieira, for their friendship, encouragement and constant support.

Many thanks for the scholarly input, leads and invigorating back and forth sharing of ideas and hunches to Dr. Mkrtich Harutyunyan, Dr. Nelli Hovhannisyan, Professor Virgílio Loureiro, Professor Manuel Malfeito Ferreira and Patrick McGovern, not forgetting wonderful on-the-ground guidance from Professor Arlindo Riuvo and José Miguel Almeida.

A final thanks to the ongoing encouragement and support from Alentejo's Comissão Vitivinícola Regional Alentejana (CVRA): ex-president Dora Simoes, for introducing me to *talha*, current president, Francisco Mateus, for broadening my experience, and the rest of the great team there for thoughts and logistical help: Tiago Caravana, Joao Barroso, Leonor Centeno and Pedro Verdial.

But the greatest acknowledgements must go to the villagers, winemakers and growers who remained true to *talha,* and who have preserved *talha's* potential for future generations.

How to read this book

In trying to ride several horses at the same time, it is easy to fall off and not please everyone, possibly anyone. Too much information will bore the socks off some readers, whereas others hoping for a highly detailed and deeper understanding of *talha* culture will always want ever more impeccably accurate information.

On one level I hope to map out a guide to *talha* wine and lay out a brief biographical history of current producers. On another I hope to delve into as much as I know and don't know about *talha* culture, infusing this throughout a narrative of the decade I've spent exploring the subject. Most of this has been gathered orally through interviews and snippets of conversations, some through sources I've read along the way and can't remember where I found it. Poor scholarship I know, but I also don't want to weigh the text down with endless footnotes, although I have tried to credit others' views where I could. I've also opted to include lots of speculation and questions I have about things no one has yet found definitive answers for, hoping it might spur someone else to finish that work.

Originally my wife Jenny and I had intended to whip out a quick ebook anyone could use on their phones as a self-guide to *talha* wine producers and the regions they live in. Where to eat, what to see, what to taste for; wine tourism based around an endangered wine culture that was frozen in time, but has miraculously thawed itself out and is now thriving in unforeseen ways. But this risked not passing on a much deeper story that deserves telling; one of lost and found technology and cultural resurrection. In the end, we've mashed it all together hoping the reader can pick and choose what they find useful.

So how to read this? There are three main sections. The first is full of background information and esoteric geeky wine and cultural stuff I love as a former historian. The second part explores individual producers and their wine in relative detail, to guide readers to the wines they may want to taste or wineries they may want to visit. The third part is more oriented towards the wine tourist. What to eat, where to stay and what to do beyond drinking.

Take your pick!

PART I: FOR THE OENOPHILE

Tilting at Oxymorons

Before digging any deeper into Talha Tales, we need to clear up a major problem with the general catch-all term 'amphora' that's commonly used for wine made in clay pots.

Some time in the recent past, some unknown someone tagged this method of winemaking incorrectly. The so-called Modern Amphora wine movement is fundamentally an oxymoron that shouldn't be.

And that's because amphora were never used during the Roman era to make wine. These long, slender, pointy, two-handled clay pots were used EXCLUSIVELY for transportation, NOT FERMENTATION.

Historically pots used for fermentation, maturation and storage were much larger, rounder and considerably harder to move. The correct name for these pots are Roman *dolia*, Georgian *qvevri*, Armenian *karas*, Spanish *tinajas* or Portuguese *talha*.

Unfortunately, 'amphora' has stuck and we continue to be stuck with it, and no amount of my endless finger-wagging and pious correcting is likely to change that.

Nevertheless, 'terracotta' or simply 'clay pot' winemaking are better, more accurate, generic terms.

So those are what I'll stick to when not being more specific.

Chapter One
Gato's Last Tasca

Leaving behind the sweltering southern Portuguese sun beating down on the sleepy little Alentejo village of Arcos, I pulled apart a clattering string of anti-fly beads hanging over an unmarked door and entered. I was in Arcos's last remaining *tasca*.

The scene was not unlike one from Pompeii, days before it met its fateful ending. The cool, narrow room had barely enough space to swing a cat, let alone for its two tiny tables. A couple of old men hunched over one, talking intensely, leaning back momentarily as the owner delivered a plate of *petiscos* (Portuguese style tapas). On the opposite wall stood my reason for being there: a couple of giant, egg-shaped clay pots (*talha* in Portuguese, pronounced somewhere between *tal-ha* and *tal-yah*).

Talha, like these, had been used for making wine in this part of Portugal continually since Roman times - perhaps longer.

I sat down. Taking a small straight-sided water glass off the shelf, 65-year-old owner Antonio Gato bent down near ground level and twisted a tiny cork that was stoppering the *talha*. Filling the glass to the brim, he offered me its golden liquid.

Antonio Gato in his *tasca*

It was like no wine I'd tasted before: relentlessly mineral, a touch honeyed with a hint of aniseed, its full body cut through with firm, fine tannins and just a whisper of acidity. It was white wine pretending to be red. Half expecting his red to be rough and rustic, surprisingly it had the freshness of Beaujolais Nouveau, but more developed, fuller-bodied, softer and much more richly-fruited. Both were easily the best twenty-five cents I'd ever spent. I was drinking history on the cheap!

Although Senhor Gato's little neighborhood *tasca* was only officially licensed in 1930, its traditional offerings and winemaking practices stretch back deeply into an unrecorded past...the ancient vinous answer to the modern brew pub.

Every September Antonio's café would close down, and the *talha* would be cleaned and resurfaced inside with a fresh mixture of *pés* (pronounced pesh). Soon the new batch of grapes would arrive from the surrounding vineyards to be crushed, with both must and skins, filling the *talha*. Fermentation would burble away naturally for a couple of weeks, and when finished, a micro-thin layer of olive oil would be added to the surface to protect the new wine from oxidation. No need for sulphur or filtration, this was a winemaker's answer to 'set and forget,' one-pot, slow cooking.

Gato, and other villagers making wine only for family use, would leave the wine to mature until St. Martin's Day: November 11. Soon after, *talhas* within the village would be tapped for the first taste of the vintage. The ensuing festivities would carry on into the early morning and weeks that followed.

By the time I first visited Antonio Gato's *tasca* over a decade ago, these traditions were already coming to an end. More worrying, the greater *talha* winemaking tradition was on the knife edge of extinction.

The old, mixed vine, field-blended grape varieties common in the past had been replaced, in Gato's case, with just two whites, Roupeiro and Rabo de Ovelha, and two reds, Alicante Bouschet and Aragonez (Tempranillo); the latter beating Beaujolais Nouveau Day to the punch by centuries.

A more disturbing development was the steady downward spiral in small-scale wine production like his, and the likelihood that Gato would be the last to carry on his ancestors' tradition. Northerners used to stop by and fill 20-liter jugs on their way home from holidaying along the Algarve, but this ended as they increasingly opted to buy bag-in-box from their local supermarkets. The modern taste for fresher, fruitier wine and flamboyant oak-barrel characters furthered the steady decline in sales.

No one was interested in continuing Gato's *tasca* after he retired. The half dozen *talha* in his annex across the street sat empty. The *tasca's* working pots were making just enough to carry his last remaining customers through the next vintage. *Tascas* had become a dying breed.

Sadly, Gato's *tasca* is now closed - although hopefully not forever.

Because *talha* wine is in the midst of a Renaissance that will ensure its survival far into the future…

Chapter Two
Talha: A Perfect Winemaking Machine

The First Time

Remembering the first time I faced one of these magnificent old winemaking pots, purely from a technological standpoint, it was stunning how brilliantly simple, indeed beautiful, the formal composition was: a funnel, atop a globe, set into a cone. Dump crushed grapes into the top, wait a couple of months for fermentation and gravity to do their work, then drain crystal-clear wine from a hole at the bottom. Drink up until empty, repeat yearly...for centuries...for millennia.

Mother *Mae*...the guts of the matter

The grapes introduced are transformed into wine with very pure grape characters, derived only from pulp, skins and native yeast. No need for chemical additions, nor artificial filtering. *Talha* are the vinous equivalent of 'three chords and the truth.'

Compared to modern winemaking technology and practices, *talha* offer similar positives without their downsides. *Talha* essentially preserve the fruit purity created by stainless steel's neutral fermentation, but without metal-made wine's sharp-edged rawness. Countering steel's negatives, *talha's* porous walls let in just enough oxygen to burnish textures and soften tannins, replicating the transformative micro-oxygenation produced by oak barrels, but - and this is a big, significant but - without oak's intrusive aromas, flavors and tannins. Purity remains undone.

Talha winemaking is relatively hands-off and gravity-driven. Bitter seeds sink to the lowest point in the pot's V, the percolating wine protected from their astringency by a covering of skins and dead yeast cells (*lees*). Internal convection currents inside a curvaceous potbelly naturally stir yeast lees, ensuring labor-free, batonless *bâtonnage*.

From an ecological standpoint, once the initial CO2 expenditure of firing the pots is paid up, thereafter the vessel shouldn't need replacement for centuries. *Talhas* do not require electricity for cooling, instead using evaporative water applied externally, to lower fermentation and maturation temperatures by as much as 20°C/36°F.

Weighing all this up, *talhas* seem to lack all the faults of modern winemaking vessels while offering a distinct set of advantages. And this is delivered through one pretty cool piece of ancient technology, which ironically, just happens to be the world's newest winemaking machine!

Forward through the past

Going back to the turn of the last millennium, not many of us realized wine could be made in clay pots, let alone that such wine would be even marginally palatable to our modern taste. At that point, the modern 'amphora' wine movement, based around northern Italy's Josko Gravner, had barely been conceived and was just beginning its earliest explorations of what might be possible. Archaeologists were still in the first stages of digging up evidence of the earliest terracotta winemaking pots associated with ancient Georgian, Armenian, Phoenician, Greek and Roman winemaking cultures.

Although modern day Georgia maintained a continuous clay pot winemaking tradition going back 6000-8000 years, few outside of that country knew much about it. Fewer still knew anything about Portugal's well-hidden *talha* secret, linking back to Roman wine.

My first conscious encounter with clay-made wine was in southern Italy's Campania region in the mid-2000s. There, Luigi Tecce was puzzling out how to make wine from the Aglianico grape, using both ancient Greek and Roman recipes, and fermenting in two different styles of terracotta pots from each ancient culture. His experimental Aglianico was as convincingly good as anything I'd had from conventionally-made Aglianico from either the Vulture or Taurasi regions. Actually, it was more interesting. It made me realize the ancients, with their so-called 'primitive' technology, had the capacity to make quite excellent wine.

Like many modern attempts at terracotta winemaking I've observed first hand since then in Istria, Croatia, Slovenia, Friuli, South Africa and more, Luigi's work involved interpreting somewhat vague instructions from ancient Roman and Greek texts, a fair bit of guesswork and a whole lot of trial and error.

Antonio Gato's wine, on the other hand, was like a living fossil, handed down through generations, with a clear, direct lineage going straight back to the earliest days of Roman winemaking. The knowledge was still there and being shared.

The Georgians too have an unbroken multi-thousand-year history of *qvevri* clay pot winemaking. But the northern Caucasus's *qvevri* traditions differ fundamentally from *talha's* southern Mediterranean traditions. The irony is that when Gravner and his fellow northern Italians attempted to relearn how to make 'Roman-like' wine in amphora, they had no idea that a genuine Roman tradition had survived intact in Alentejo. Instead, they adopted the traditional practices of Georgian *qvevri* as their model.

Although all terracotta technology and winemaking practices share many similarities, there are significant differences between *qvevri* and *talha*, resulting in quite different wine styles.

The biggest technological differences are that *qvevri* are buried underground, sealed at the top with damp clay for six months and thereafter drained with a bucket from the top. *Talha* are free-standing, sealed with a top layer of olive oil to protect against oxidation and, cleverly, are drained via gravity through taps at their base.

Stylistically the major difference, apart from the grapes used, is that *qvevri* wine is kept on its skins for six months, which makes it considerably more tannic (astringent) than *talha* wine, which only has two to three months of skin contact and is ready to drink earlier.

After repeated trips to both Georgia and Alentejo, I came to view *qvevri* and *talha* as the beginning and ending of the evolutionary refinement of clay pot winemaking technology over a 4000-6000 year period; stretching from *qvevri*'s antiquarian origins, through to *talha*'s supposed birth around 2000 years ago and the perfection of terracotta as a winemaking vessel.

Fortunately for the Georgians, *qvevri* traditions remain very much alive and healthy, and central to Georgian winemaking culture. Less fortunately, at that point, Portugal's ancient unbroken *talha* traditions were considerably less secure.

When I first began searching out *talha*-made wines back around 2010, and finally tasted some in 2012, there were just a handful of *tascas* and family producers still active, another handful of professional winemakers focused on Alentejo's relatively new Vinho de Talha DOC designation, and one quixotic attempt to resurrect factory scale production.

All were actively trying to keep *talha* traditions alive. It was a precarious situation with *talha* barely holding on by its proverbial finger nails, dangerously on the edge of extinction.

Chapter Three
Talha's Resurrection

The Rebirth

Talha began sneaking into my brain around 2010. It would eventually develop into a throbbing *idée fixe*. Before that I had heard little snippets about families still making wine in clay pots like the Romans did, down in a handful of remote villages in the middle of Alentejo. A tradition that, while long gone elsewhere, was, against all odds, somehow surviving.

These were some of the poorest parts of Portugal: dusty, depressed, half-emptied of people and opportunity. Places where time hadn't just stood still, it had slipped backward. Exactly the sort of places where ancient unbroken Roman traditions might still be hanging on by a thread. A thread that could snap at any moment. I knew I had to see this old tradition first-hand before it vanished forever.

And so I started pestering the then-president of Alentejo's Comissão Vitivinícola Regional Alentejana (CVRA), Dora Simoes. Like all of Portugal's other wine regions, Alentejo's CVR was in charge of regulating and promoting their local region's wine industry. Its primary role was to protect the reputation of the region's wines by certifying a level of quality consumers could count on. Equally important, they helped producers to market and sell the wine they made.

Simoes was one of Portuguese wine's most progressive managers. Between her deep understanding of the wine industry from the inside out, and the highly organized team she had brought together, Alentejo's CVR had done much to elevate the region's wine reputation globally.

The first few times I mentioned my interest in seeing *talha* and tasting the wines, Dora would quietly change the subject or divert my attention to something else. Eventually she alluded to things being worked out behind the scenes and that my request might be possible in future. I told her I didn't mind if the wines were a bit rough and rustic, it was mainly to satisfy my curiosity about the lineage going back to Roman times.

Little did I know then that a local *talha* activist group of fifteen allied winemakers, co-branding themselves as Vitifrades, was in the process of negotiating with CVR to create an official Alentejo Vinho de Talha DOC (*Denominacão de Origen Controlada*) designation. The association had been established in 1998, within the parish of Vila de Frades, to promote and protect traditional *talha*-made wine. The negotiating team included Vila de Frades's Arlindo Ruivo, Vidigueira Cooperativa's chairman, José Miguel Almeida, and Oscar Gato (Antonio Gato's nephew) who represented the northern *talha* traditions and was winemaker for Borba's cooperative. Advising them in the background was the University of Lisboa's Dr. Virgilio Loueiro, Portugal's leading wine historian and a passionate believer in Portuguese traditional approaches to wine.

All were deeply committed to the formal recognition of Alentejo's - if not Iberia's - oldest, purest and most distinctive style of wine.

On the other side of the discussions, Dora and the CVR were just as actively involved in ensuring the quality of *talha* wine, while at the same time protecting both its potential growth and the reputation of all Alentejo wine from anything that might be considered, at that point, sub-standard. *Talha* wine still had a lot to prove in terms of quality, consistency and how it could slot into the modern world.

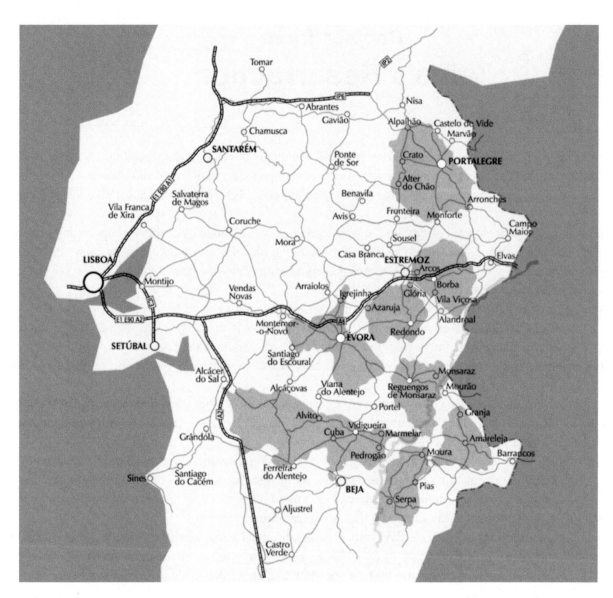

Alentejo DOC regions: from from top to bottom:
Portalegre, Borba, Redondo, Evora, Reguengos, Vidigueira, Granja-Amareleja, and Moura.
Map provided by CVRA.

In retrospect how this came together was quite an accomplishment, since nowhere else on earth had any wine regulatory body ever 'officially' sanctioned an ancient method of wine production before. Nor since, for that matter. France's *Appellation d'Origine Contrôlée* system (AOC) hadn't considered it, nor Spain's nor Italy's nor anywhere else in the New or Old World.

All this was made all the more difficult because it flew in the face of the world's current squeaky clean, technology-driven, science-based approach to winemaking (refrigerated stainless steel tanks, inoculated yeasts, new oak maturation, enzyme and chemical additions, etc). Everyone concerned was in uncharted territory.

Eventually, DOC status was granted in 2010, with the first DOC wines set for certification in 2011. The rules were kept clear-cut and relatively simple, more or less, following Alentejo's traditional *talha* formula. The grapes had to be grown and the wine made within one of Alentejo's designated subregions: Portalegre, Borba, Redondo, Evora, Reguengos, Vidigueira, Granja/Amareleja, and Moura, and only from officially sanctioned varieties.

The wine had to be made in a *talha* (defined as an impermeable waterproofed pot). All the grapes had to be destemmed, thereafter the skins and pulp went into *talha* and the resultant fermented wine and residual *mae* (mother in English) had to be kept intact until St. Martin's Day (November 11).

Certification could only happen from that date, following an official inspection that proved the wine had not been removed from the intact mother still residing inside the pot. In a gesture to quality control, the wines, like all other Alentejo DOC wines, had to meet the minimum organoleptic requirements regarding color, clarity, aroma and flavor. In short, the wines had to be fault-free and taste good.

Showtime!

After all the regulations had been worked out and were settling in, my chance to experience this up close arrived in 2012. Simoes planned a whirlwind tour of *talha* culture.

Starting out with Senhor Gato's typical *tasca*, she followed on with Iberia's largest Roman-era winemaking complex, Villa Romana de São Cucufate. Then, just around a hill, we moved on to the nearby village of Vila de Frades (village of friars), where she introduced me to the venerable keeper of the faith, Professor Arlindo Ruivo and his living museum. A couple of streets over, I watched a small band of *talha's* well seasoned warriors, Vitifrades, fill their pots with the new vintage. And then we lunched at Pais das Uvas, one of a couple of surviving *talha*-focused, family run *taberna* restaurants. To cap it all off, we moved on to the finale, *talha's* grand cathedral, Jose de Sousa.

In just a few intense days, Simoes had laid out the entire gamut of *talha* culture for me, encapsulating its evolution through its oldest to newest periods, and from modest, everyday levels through to the grandest designs. I met its localized, inwardly-focused champions, intent on preserving what they had before it was gone, and a singular visionary outsider, focused outwardly on how equally important it was to take *talha* into the world beyond to capture a much wider audience - one receptive to its message, and that had the potential to support its survival and growth into a brighter future.

But little did I realize I'd only scratched the surface…

São Cucufate

São Cucufate is the anchor in this story. All roads lead back to São Cucufate, just as they had once led away.

São Cucufate is the largest surviving Roman villa in all of Iberia

It is a magnificent ruin, the largest surviving Roman villa in all of Iberia (see Tourist section). Purposefully built in the 1st century AD as a farming complex, its success allowed a wealthy farmer to construct a grand villa atop, and a Roman temple off to the side. Ongoing success allowed continual expansion for another 300 years.

Right from the start wine was made there, evidenced by the three Roman *dolia* (wine fermentation pots) excavated in the 1970s. Fossilized grape seeds, vine pruners, wine presses and amphora (for transporting) were also found. Cucufate's thick walls and high barrel-vaulted ceilings created a cool and dark space perfect for fermentation and wine storage. Alongside this, outside and just above, was a sophisticated, pre-processing system; *lagars* for foot treading, and stone presses. Any modern winemaker would envy this clever, highly efficient, naturally-cooled, gravity-fed system.

It is thought now that wine wasn't primarily consumed locally, instead it was destined for Pax Julia (modern Beja) about a day's delivery ride away by oxcart. There it may have served local taverns or was warehoused for export beyond, possibly to Rome itself. The wine and grape-growing must have been good because the Romans tagged the surrounding region with a wine-related name, Vitigeria. The name survives in the nearby village of Vidigueira.

It's still unclear if the Romans were the first to plant grapes and make wine in the region, considering the Pheonicians were in the area before, and the local tribes before them are likely to have made wine. The verdict is still out.

By any standards, it's an old, old place. Cucufate sits atop an earlier Neolithic habitation. Somewhere between a half a mile and a kilometer away, the sky is pierced by a 4000-6000 year old phallic-like megalith, *Menhir of Mac Abraham*...no doubt, someone or someones must have danced, sung and shared a cup of grog around this in the past. A couple of miles beyond is a lengthy Roman bridge over an old dried up river leading to an old silted up Roman dam. Nearby in Vidigueira (pop. 6,000), there's evidence of a smaller ruined Roman farmhouse, *Insuínha II*, which also included a wine press and cellar.

After the fall of Rome in the 5th century it's unclear what happened during the barbarian invasion from the north. But you would think any self-respecting barbarian wouldn't discourage ongoing wine production. Wine was definitely produced during the following Visigoth occupation and their early Christian era in the 600s. A monastery, named for Saint Cucufate, was established sometime between the 7th and 10th centuries (possibly by Augustinians, Benedictines or Capuchins), and that probably continued through the Islamic occupation after 830AD, with a possible interruption during the violent Christian reconquest in the 1100s. Documentation picks up again in 1255 when a new monastery, church and village of Vila de Frades were established by friars from Lisbon's São Vicente de Fora in the ruins, based on the fame of wine quality within the surrounding Vidigueira region at that point. Although some monks continued making wine there up through the 15th century and perhaps after, most had steadily shifted to live in Vila de Frades by that time. (see wikipedia, https://pt.wikipedia.org/wiki/Vila_de_Frades).

Cucufate remains central to *talha* culture. It's still an easy walk - remembering back to the days when people walked everywhere - to *talha* culture's last holdout villages: Vila de Frades, Vidigueira, Cuba and Vila Alva - *Talha's* Ground Zero.

The Professor

A key reference point for *talhas* in Vila de Frades and greater *talha* culture is Professor Arlindo Ruivo (see also Gerações de Talha in the Producers section). Following his retirement as a local school teacher, Ruivo has become a font of practical knowledge and oral history concerning local *talha* production stretching back deep into the 20th century. Much of this was gathered first-hand after taking over his family's *talha* wine production in the early 1990s. He is well loved locally, where he is respectfully called 'The Professor'.

Since then he has kept his hand in, making enough wine for family and friends. Undoubtedly his most important role has been helping to keep *talha* tradition alive during its darkest days of decline, himself ever happy to explain to anyone interested in *talha,* while biding his time until the next generation was eager to grab the baton and take it forward into the future.

Ruivo's Aladdin's cave of *Talha* paraphernalia

My first visit to his wonderfully cluttered, rust-and-dust-filled cellar, jam-packed full of essential *talha* paraphernalia, was a joy to the eyes. Purpose-built in the 17th century as a producing cellar, it has vaulted ceilings that echo nearby São Cucufate's arched chapel. Deceptively larger than it seemed initially, I counted roughly forty large *talhas* tucked away in its cool, dark alcoves, suggesting peak production was once around 30,000-40,000 liters. In fact, he recalled that during the early-to-mid-20th century the adega had produced around 30,000 liters of wine, mostly from white Antão Vaz grapes and sold in small barrels to restaurants and shops throughout the Beja region. Echos of Cucufate.

One of my first questions concerned the mysterious stuff known as *pés* that Senhor Gato had mentioned was used to coat the inside of *talha.* This appeared to have become a lost art, since no one made it themselves or seemed to agree how it was made. Traditional *pés* was clearly a complex concoction.

Ruivo remembered, as did Gato, and many others related later, the time when almost every family in the village had a *talha* and their own secret *pés* recipe. It was possible to taste a wine back then and from its *pés* character alone, guess who made it.

His recollection was that the basis was rosemary, thyme, pine-nut tree resin, and olive oil, all carefully boiled together to a stage where it 'wasn't too liquid or too solid.' This Goldilocks Point ensured resin characters didn't dominate the wine. Like Gato, he also remembered specialist *pesgadores* who moved from village to village inverting *talhas* over fires to melt out the old *pés* linings, then scrubbing the *talhas* with fennel, and recoating (see To *Pés* or not to *Pés* chapter). It sounded complicated, if not cumbersome, but much easier than how the Georgians cleaned or renewed their buried *qvevri.*

I revisited Professor Arlindo's magical emporium to *talha* culture almost yearly thereafter and always walked away with some newly discovered tidbit to add to my knowledge.

The Brotherhood

Just a couple of streets over, Simoes took me to see some of the Vitifrades team filling a *talha* with the new vintage. This time the setting was less romantic, but no less passionate. Their adega was ensconced in a sterile, squarish, garage-like building; fitting for a band of *talha* garagistas. Outside sat a pickup truck with its bed full of freshly picked grapes. These were being fed into a noisy crusher attached to an equally noisy electric pump that sucked the shredded grapes and skins into a fat, brightly-colored plastic hose, shunting them ever upward, eventually splashing their contents into a couple of head-high *talha*. Although the contrast between old and new was discordant, it was also reassuring.

There I met Vitifrades' long term president, José Miguel Almeida, and a PR guy who was snapping photos for the next Facebook post. Almeida offered me last year's vintage to taste, which was still freshly crisp and remarkably good.

Taking pride of place on a sawhorse table sat a newly designed bottle, just for Vinho de Talha DOC wines. Made out of terracotta and shaped like a squat, flat-topped *talha*, it truly did look the part. Unfortunately, because it could only hold a tiny short cork, it eventually proved impractical and was abandoned the following year. Nevertheless, it seemed a good idea at the time and looked great.

It is worth noting that Almeida is also chairman of Adega Cooperativa Vidigueira, Cuba and Alvito, which includes Vila de Frades within its boundaries. The cooperative's 300 members currently farm 15,000 hectares of vines, every one of which would probably have gone into *talha* wine before the cooperative was founded in 1960. A similar situation would have existed with the Cooperativa Adega de Borba, and Alentejo's other regional cooperatives established between the 1940s and 60s. Collectively, the ancestors of the families who send their grapes to these cooperatives today were the heart and soul of *talha* culture.

You Don't Know What You Got Till It's Gone

Although these cooperatives and many of their individual members have played an active role in continuing *talha* culture in recent times, the co-ops inadvertently played a major role in *talha's* historical decline and near extinction.

In previous times, going back centuries, the life of a vigneron (a grape-grower who makes wine) was often precarious: weather could be difficult (drought, rain, frost, hail), resulting in crop failure or poor quality grapes. Selling to a wider market was rarely simple. In the best of times income could be marginal, while at the worst, barely subsistent.

Cooperatives were formed primarily to help *talha* wine producers focus on grape-growing, rather than the more 'iffy' parts of the equation: making, marketing, selling, distribution, etc. They offered professionally-trained winemaking teams, modern technologies, economies of scale, centralized sales and, most importantly, a steady, secure income.

Cooperatives also provided something *talha* couldn't: longevity. *Talha* wine was the stuff of shooting stars, bright and beautiful, then suddenly gone. It was meant to be drunk fresh, straight from *talha*, as in Gato's *tasca*. As summer's heat increased, *talha* wine could go off, turning into vinegar or worse. By the 1970s, cooperatives were able to bottle wine so that it could consistently last for years. And that changed everything forever.

It is little wonder then that where once there were hundreds, if not thousands, of local *talha* winemakers, suddenly they flowed en-masse into cooperative production. There were other advantages to this beyond financial security. Families still had the option to retain a small pot or two for family consumption, but shifting the bulk of their production away from home allowed them to reclaim newly-emptied cellar space for more room to live in: a win-win all round.

The darker side of all this created a snowball effect. The remaining *talha* producers would have been steadily undercut on price and increasingly forced out of business by cheaper, more modern styles of co-op wine. So goes the inevitable flow of 'progress.'

By the 1990s, *talha* winemaking teetered on the edge of extinction, barely kept alive by a handful of (mostly old) people and their living memories of what had been.

An increasing recognition of this loss energized some in the cooperative community to reclaim their heritage, inspiring the initial activism that fought to save small-scale *talha* winemaking that kept families in everyday wine and *tabernas* at the center of village social life.

All of which gave rise to the Vitifrades group and various allied supporters. Their aim was the preservation of their own local *talha* culture, the establishment of Vinho de Talha DOC within CVR's jurisdiction, and the eventual elevation of *talha* wines to a special status within Alentejo's current production.

Talha's Cathedral

Paralleling the hundreds, if not thousands, of urban-based *talha* adegas in the past, were grander rural estates and suburban wineries making *talha* wine on considerably larger scales - the modern equivalent of the large Roman villa and factory-farm production found at São Cucufate.

Jose de Sousa's magnificent *Talha* cellar - the cathedral of *talha*

Another way to view them is as the precursors of the modern, highly-efficient, massive production facilities that dominate global winemaking today: the Gallos, Antinoris and Penfolds of another era.

Historically only a handful of these large *talha* wine producers existed in Alentejo during the 19th and early 20th centuries. The most revered were rural estates like Mouchao, Tapata do Chaves, Carmo (now Dona Maria) and urban-based Jose de Sousa. Of these iconic wineries, ONLY Jose de Sousa continued with *talha* production throughout the 20th century and into the 21st.

Casa Agrícola José de Sousa Rosado Fernandes, and its nearby vineyards at Herdade do Monte da Ribeira, shifted their previous farmhouse production to a new 'modern' adega on the outskirts of Reguengos de Monsaraz in 1878. In its heyday the cellar housed around one hundred and twenty 1500+ liter/400 gallon *talhas*, plus enough 3000-5000-liter chestnut barrels to mature the wine their *talha* produced. In modern terms, production may have reached well over 100,000 bottles.

Long revered as one of Alentejo's greatest producers, many of Jose de Sousa's *talha*-made red wines are legendary. Indeed, it's still possible to find local restaurants serving wonderfully drinkable bottles going back to the 1940s; many of which have been cellared on-site since their release. The fact that 80-year-old *talha* wines (see Jose de Sousa section) are still drinking well is a testament to both the winery and the technology that produced it. These are by far the oldest surviving clay pot-produced wines anywhere in the world today.

The story behind Jose de Sousa's survival into the present, follows a trail of decay, death and resurrection.

After thriving throughout most of its lifetime, the 1970s proved to be a difficult period for Casa Agrícola José de Sousa Rosado Fernandes. When the owner died early in the decade, ownership passed to his wife, and after her death, to a nephew with no interest in wine. Hands-on production fell to a well-meaning consultant with relatively little experience or understanding of *talha* wine production. The resulting wines were inconsistent at best, and undrinkable at worst.

Compounding problems, the 1974 revolution brought a communist takeover of the Herdade's old vineyard. The new worker-owners failed to prune for several years, then, when they did, scarred the old vines so badly they almost died off.

Between the two, by the 1980s, José de Sousa's wine quality had steadily spiralled downward into irretrievable decadence. The adega's sudden death came after three workers died of CO_2 asphyxiation while cleaning out concrete storage tanks during the 1984 vintage. Soon after, the adega was up for sale.

Resurrection followed, when one of Portugal's largest and more progressive producers José Maria da Fonseca purchased Casa Agrícola José de Sousa Rosado Fernandes in 1986. Fortunately, Fonseca's University of Davis-trained chief winemaker, Domingos Soares Franco, had a deep respect for its *talha* production, old wines and old vine, Grand Noir-dominant vineyards. Part of the original negotiating team, if Franco hadn't been board chairman and a Fonseca family member, this seriously decrepit, seemingly irrelevant, obviously obsolete, archaic icon (irony intended here) may never have been restored to its former glory.

This was the 1980s after all, when the wine industry's way forward wasn't interested in looking back and the past was best left where it was. 'Progressive' winemaking was locked into stainless steel, new oak barrels, chemical wizardry, temperature control and the latest technology...lots of it.

NO ONE in their right mind would want to make wine in CLAY POTS! Let alone think they could sell it to anyone! But Franco - deeply schooled in modern Californian winemaking practices - recognized that nowhere else in the world had *talha* technology. Nor a direct link back to ancient Roman winemaking. *Talha* were exclusively Portuguese and quintessentially Alentejan.

True to itself, Alentejo's path forward was through its past

After taking possession, Fonseca eventually redeveloped most of the complex into a massive, ultra-modern winemaking facility. Beyond that, Franco turned his attention toward the old adega's original cool, dark, subterranean cellar. His pet project was in a ruinous state with its original hundred and twenty *talha* capacity having dwindled to around twenty pots, many cracked and stapled back together. Standing alongside these were a couple of rows of irretrievably dilapidated 3000-5000 liter chestnut barrels previously used for storage and maturation. Dried out and heavily splintering, they were only good for firewood.

One of the first major problems faced was that Alentejo's once thriving *talha* pot-making industry had died off in the 1920s. The fact was, no one made *talha* anymore or knew how to make them, nor even knew anyone who had ever made one. *Talha* masters were as dead and deeply buried as their industry. Finding new *talha* replacements was simply not possible.

Undaunted, Franco and his team set about cleaning and restoring as many surviving *talha* as possible. Luckily, fifty were bought in from a neighbor's old adega. After searching far and wide for more replacements - antique shops, garden centers, lawn decorations, etc…they eventually amassed around 114 *talha*. All were pre-1930, ranging in size from 300-2000 liters. Many were identifiably produced between 1819-1908 and visibly branded by master craftsmen from nearby Sao Pedro do Corval (formerly named Aldeia do Mato), Campo Maior and Vidigueira.

Equally important was the restoration of lost intellectual capital. There were no instruction books or teachers to turn to for help in knowing how Jose de Sousa had made wine in the past. As all of Jose de Sousa's old wine stock had been sold off previously, Franco didn't have a lot to draw on in terms of deconstructing wine styles, let alone reproducing what grape blend went into the adega's 'house' wine style, Rosado Fernandes.

But eventually Franco located the adega's long-retired, 80-year-old cellar master. Drawing from his first-hand knowledge of the adega's 1950-60s golden age, Franco began piecing together both common and extraordinary pre-1960s practices.

Importantly, a library of over one hundred old wines going back to the 1940s was reassembled through auctions and swapping 'new for old' with local restaurants' cellar stocks.

Franco and his team weren't flying blind now.

The first few vintages were driven by trial and error, with production beginning to come back on track by 1988. The following years were spent understanding the technology in its own right, rather than trying to 'improve' it with modern winemaking concepts.

One of the first lessons learned was that *talha* demand serious respect. Apart from the danger of CO2 asphyxiation, *talha* can become lethal bombs. In the early days, it was not unusual for Franco to open the cellar doors in the morning to find that overnight a fermenting *talha* had exploded, tossing massive 50mm/2inch-thick shards of clay a good 10 meters/yards away. The problem was that carbon dioxide (CO2) from fermentation had built up under a tightly sealed surface 'cap' of grape skins wedged into the *talha*'s throat. Franco recalls one such kaboom just seconds away from opening a door handle. A few ruined *talha* - and near misses - later, a solution was found. This required cellar men round the clock on 'punch down' duty, regularly breaking up the cap to alleviate any deadly pressure from building up.

Beyond dodging sudden death, Franco, schooled in cutting edge modern technological practice, was slowly understanding how to unlock some of the more sophisticated secrets of clay pot winemaking.

One of *talha*'s cleverest technological advantages over Georgia's 'buried pot' *qvevri* technology proved to be an ability to control temperature naturally via evaporation. Simply pouring water across a *talha*'s big, broad belly can lower fermentation temperatures from 30-40 degrees centigrade (86-104 F), way down to 18-20 degrees (64-58 F) - measurably below what's desirable for red wine production. Achieving similar results in modern stainless steel tank winemaking requires electricity, gas coolants for refrigeration, wires, plugs, dials and utility bills.

All a *talha* needs is free, non-polluting water, applied as, where and when desired.

Odd little discoveries continued to pop up over time. Like the practical reason behind what, perplexingly, seemed to be an oddly decorative, raised, rope-like ring around the top of each *talha*'s collar. Certainly it looked good, but it turns out this plays a central role in controlling the *talha*'s inbuilt heat exchange system. Water, poured from above the ring, twists into rivulets that are evenly distributed across the *talha's* belly during fermentation. Franco's team learned to fine-tune this to the fermentation temperature requirements for each vintage.

Similarly, the clay's rough, unfinished surface appeared to be purposeful, helping to slow and capture water, further amplifying cooling. Beyond fermentation, water cooling also helped to maintain consistent maturation temperatures within the adega during summertime spikes. (All this begs for a comparative carbon-neutral study pegging *talha* against less efficient, less consistent, electrically-driven, refrigerator-clad, stainless steel tanks. Bets on the winner?)

Perhaps the most brilliant aspect of *talha* is its natural, gravity fed, filtration system. This is constructed around grape stems placed into the *talha's* lowest point. After fermentation, gravity pulls bitter seeds to the very bottom, then dead yeast lees settle atop, thus protecting wine from unwanted bitterness. Thereafter a further layer of skin and lees sediment settles above, providing a natural filter. Franco discovered how efficient this was quite unexpectedly, when draining his first finished wine through a hole at the *talha's* base. Whereas the initial 20 liters (5ish US gallons) of wine was cloudy, it quickly ran clear for the remaining 1000+ liters. After returning the first cloudy 20 liters to the top, this eventually filtered through cleanly as well.

The more practical 'hands on' experience Franco racked up, the deeper his respect grew for the brilliance of *talha's* inbuilt technology. Every aspect of form, shape and size was proving purposeful. And where clay may have seemed primitive and simple to others, it was clearly very very clever in its technological simplicity.

Points of Difference

Historically, Jose de Sousa's expansive *talha* winemaking facility had two major differences compared to smaller, village-based 'all in one' *talha* production. These were: pre-*talha* processing in large stone, rectangular shaped *lagars*, and post-fermentation maturation in large wooden barrels.

At grape entry, street level, Jose de Sousa's old cellar contains two massive stone *lagars* designed for foot-treading grapes into must, which then drains via gravity into *talha* located on a subterranean level below. Large granite *lagars* are more normally considered a northern Portuguese winemaking technology. However, many of Alentejo's larger producers, including São Cucufate, had a similar set up, although these tended to be made of marble rather than the north's granite.

Lagars offer a wide variety of winemaking options not available in simple, all in one pot, *talha* production. One key aspect of production is that grapes must be completely crushed before going into *talha* to avoid carbonic maceration and reduce CO_2 build up. Where small family/*taberna*-sized production crushed grapes directly into *talha* for fermentation, *lagars* created an optional processing step before this. *Lagars* allow destemmed grapes to be more gently crushed by foot (instead of harsher shredding in a mechanical crusher), ensuring softer tannin extraction as well as more thorough integration of fruit, acidity and tannins. All this could be done prior to going into *talha* for fermentation.

Lagars can also replicate a modern winemaking practice called 'cold soak' or pre-fermentation maceration. This entails dumping intact grape berries in *lagars* and then delaying foot treading for a day or so. This lets them stew in their own juice for a bit, where each individual grape becomes its own fermentation vessel developing an early stage of low-level carbonic maceration. Thereafter, pre-softened grapes are stomped and sent to *talha* for fermentation. This kind of pre-processing enhances aromatics, fruitiness, and mouthfeel and softens tannins. It also allows the yeast to breathe a bit, reproduce, and develop a healthy fermentation.

A third option, common in northern Portugal, is to either partially or fully ferment stomped grapes in the *lagar*, where fermentation creates a fog-like blanket of CO_2 hovering over the new wine, protecting it from oxidation. After full or partial fermentation this wine can be moved into *talha* or barrels for further ageing.

Cellarmen using a *ripanco* to hand crush grapes into a *lagar*

Any of these processes, alone or in various combinations, can create quite distinctive *talha* wine styles, resulting in different aromas, flavors, textures and tannic structure. All possibilities would have been available to Jose de Sousa and Alentejo's other historic larger producers in the past.

In the early days, Franco systematically experimented with all of these *lagar*-to-*talha* combinations. Back in 2014, I had the chance to taste some of these experimental wines 'blind.' Each was made from Grand Noir grapes (a crossing of Aramond Noir and Petit Bouschet), but fermented differently.

The first (foot-trodden then *talha*-fermented) presented soft, savory dried fruit, mushroom-like aromas and flavors with a touch of spice. Complete, nicely integrated and continuous in the mouth, structurally it was clean, well delineated, with firm tannins.

A second wine was fermented only in *lagar* then moved to *talha* to mature. This offered very broad floral aromas with strong leafy/stem notes. Rounder and more consolidated texturally, surprisingly, its tannins were much softer.

The third was a control wine, fermented in modern stainless steel tanks. It had chocolate/ mocha aromas and peppery, leafy florals - sitting somewhere between the others aromatically, but considerably less integrated; rawer to be frank, with much sharper acids and tannins.

One intriguing piece of technology inherited in Jose de Sousa's chattels was an old, slatted wooden, washboard-like, destemming table, placed over *lagars*. Called *ripanco*, counter to modern practice, it was used to shred stems as well. The older retired cellarman told Franco that after separating stems from skins, the stems were crushed again separately and that juice was fermented in small 300 liter *talha* (called *tareco*) to super-concentrate tannins. This astringent *ripanco* concoction was used like 'salt and pepper' to season the wine, back-blending it into the larger pots after fermentation to adjust tannic structure; an early, more natural, form of Australia's much loved, powdered tannin addition. Franco is certain this technique was used in the legendary reds from the 1940-60s eras.

Jose de Sousa's other major difference with small volume *talha* winemaking was and is wood maturation. Used almost universally throughout Portugal before the 1980s, large producers aged their wine in very large casks (*foudres*). These were commonly made from Portuguese chestnut trees or mahogany from Brazil and ranged from 3000-5000 liters, but casks up to and over 10,000 liters were not uncommon.

When Franco took possession of the adega it had a full complement of *foudre* like this, but all were long disused, either too dried out and leaky, or too dirty to bring back into production. A couple were kept for show, but the rest were thrown out or burned. Like old *talha*, they weren't produced in Portugal any more, so not easily replaced. Unfortunately, they were the one key part of the old production method that still wasn't usable at that point. Lacking this option, Franco turned to smaller French oak barriques instead.

By 1990 Fonseca had brought the old vineyard back under ownership and restored it to healthy production. Armed with as much of Jose de Sousa's traditional winemaking palette as he could muster, Franco began steadily working towards recreating the wine styles that survived from the 1940-60s.

Again, we need to consider the timescale in all this. During the late 1980s and early 1990s 'internationalist' style dominated the top levels of winemaking throughout the world. Although it was only just beginning to creep into Portugal, the prevailing trend was to reshape Portuguese wine along these internationalist lines.

Franco and the Jose de Sousa team had many challenges over and above simply making basic drinkable wine in *talha*. No one anywhere in the world was making wine in clay pots commercially and relatively few people knew it was even possible.

While it's true the Georgians made wine in *qvevri* and a handful of villagers still made *talha* in Alentejo, both were virtually unknown outside of their local areas before the 2000s. Bear in mind also that this was a good fifteen years before Josco Gravner kick-started the Italian amphora wine movement, and two decades before the establishment of Vinho de Talha DOC regulations.

As revolutionary as it actually was, selling wine made in clay pots to the world in the late 1980s and 1990s was more than an oddball novel idea. In financial terms, it was more akin to suicide.

Without exception, all of the world's greatest, most famous and most expensive wines were matured in new 225-liter/50 gallon French oak barrels. These were *de rigueur*, with styles driven by their incumbent aromas, flavors and textures. Any serious wine had to be produced in new French oak barrels. Full stop.

By the mid 1990s, Jose de Sousa was geared up to make an iconic Alentejo wine based around its own traditional technology and local grapes. Looking back to the past for inspiration and armed with three tools: *lagars, talhas* and wooden barrels, they created something completely new from something that was very old.

After experimental bottlings and a couple of CVR certified Garrafeiras in early the 1990s, Jose de Sousa settled on its *talha*-focused style. Branded Major in 1994, the wine blended Grand Noir (55%), Trincadeira (35%) and Aragonês (10%) that was foot-trodden in *lagars* with 30% stem addition. Recalling the old cellarmaster had said Jose de Sousa had used *lagars* and *talha* in tandem, Domengos sent half to *talha* for fermentation and half stayed in *lagar* to ferment. After fermentation both lots were blended together in December and transferred to French oak barrels to age for nine months.

In 2007 they added a Grand Reserve style produced only in the best vintages. Called 'J', this was made from Grand Noir (55%), Touriga Francesa (30%), Touriga Nacional (15%) exclusively from the old, original 'mixed variety 'Jose de Sousa Vineyard' planted in 1952/53. That vineyard had replanted grapes from a previous vineyard that had gone into the great Jose de Sousa wines of the 1940s. J used foot-trodden grapes in *lagars*, again with 30% stem addition, but this time fermented only in *talha* and then aged in French oak barriques for nine months.

Eventually, Franco realized French oak dominant characters weren't replicating the classic 'Rosado Fernandes' wines made in the 1940s, 50s and 60s. The transparency of *talha*-fermented fruit begged for much more neutral, large-format chestnut casks.

This gave rise to Puro Tinto which first appeared in 2015. Shedding the last vestige of 'modernism', Franco traded in French oak maturation for 600-liter chestnut casks and also added traditional Moreto grapes, which lightened and brightened up the blend. Gaining full Vinho de Talha DOC certification, it represents the culmination of a decades-long search to recreate one of *talha's* greatest wines.

After more than thirty years Domingos Soares Franco is beginning to feel like he's finally fitted in the last few puzzle pieces that produced Jose de Sousa's finest vintages.

Last time I talked with him, he felt he'd achieved what he hoped to accomplish in helping to re-establish *talha* wine's place in the future.

Nearing retirement, one could sense a tiny regret in not being around to play a role in where it will go next.

Chapter Four
Then vs Now

A lot has happened to *talha* wine since it teetered on the edge of extinction a decade ago. Portugal's ancient answer to modern 'amphora' winemaking managed a paltry 700 liters (1000 bottles) in 2010, produced by a handful of dreamy-eyed romantics trying their best to keep the last threads of Roman winemaking technology from drifting out of reach forever.

By 2021, Alentejo's production was topping out closer to 181,000 liters/240,000 bottles of 'officially' certified Vinho de Talha DOC. And that remarkable total doesn't include declassified *talha*-made 'amphora' wine, or large volumes destined to be served in the traditional way - at its best - straight from the pot in restaurants.

This book is centered around a core of seventeen of the twenty-three professional producers focused on *talha* wine. Many more are in the early stages of experimentation and set to join the ranks in coming years. Restaurants containing *talha* that once served homemade wine to customers have opened again. Families and hobbyists are once more making wine for their own consumption. Villages are holding local competitions for the best family-made *talha* wine of the year.

November's yearly Amphora Day event, held at Herdade do Rocim, has gone from 20 to 40 to 60 exhibitors, establishing it as 'ground zero' for clay pot winemakers from around the world.

Amphora Day 2022 at Herdade do Rocim - 'ground zero' event for clay pot winemakers from around the world

New *talha*-focused museums, interpretive centers and tasting rooms have opened up, creating tourist attractions. Tourists have noticed and are coming in droves. By all counts, jobs and affluence are on the rise, villages have scrubbed up, and things are looking good. *Talha* wine has been nothing short of transformative.

Back when I wrote my first *talha* article in 2015, sources on *talha* were limited. I sifted through a dearth of information, trying to piece scraps together and make sense of what I could. Much of what I learned was secondhand oral history, often highly speculative, sometimes contradictory or specific to a local or family perspective projected as universal practice. Answered questions led to more questions, often met with shrugs and smiles, because no one had an answer yet. All of which is quite fair and to be expected, given it was the early days of the revival.

What has happened since has been an explosion of knowledge and practical experience.

Back in 2012 it looked like *talha* production was as dead and done for as the last master potters who had given up their craft in the 1920s, their secrets buried with them, any thought of replication impossible. Most producers were resolved to the likelihood that future *talha* wine production was forever limited to 150 or so surviving pots

Fortunately, since then a massive amount of lost *talha* pots have reappeared, with nearly 700 pots either in use or awaiting refurbishment. A couple of new pot-makers have opened shop and are hoping to renew the profession.

Similarly, where before a question about the *pés* used to coat the interior of *talha* garnered little definitive information, beyond shrugs and speculation, now there are professionals applying *pés* and a growing body of knowledge surrounding its use.

Most significantly, whole new types and styles of *talha* wines have appeared. Vinho de Talha DOC, like the 12 Bar Blues, has evolved into a classic form in its own right, universal enough to make comparative judgments within its own genre. Other newer *talha* wine styles have evolved more along the lines of jazz, allowing both traditional and new styles to live side by side, enhancing rather than detracting from one another.

Recently one of these new *talha* wines sold out its entire production for 1000 euros a bottle - suddenly the world noticed.

Looking back a decade, it was touch and go whether *talha* wine would survive other than as a tiny, anachronistic holdout in an unknown, relatively impoverished part of a relatively unknown wine region in Southern Portugal... tain't like that no more.

Chapter Five
To Pés or not to Pés...

Many hands

The process of *pesage* is jaw-droppingly dangerous. This I observed first hand over a very long evening watching ten men at XXVI Talha's adega while they put two of their 1,200+ liter *talhas* through the process of *pesagem*. It was dramatic, sometimes breathtaking, indeed, at times both breath-holding and breath-stopping, stuff.

Many men wrestling the *talha* into position

It began suddenly with twenty well planted hands carefully tipping a *talha* - the size and weight of a family hatchback car - down from its regular position and gently resting it on its side, accompanied by anxious, gruntily shouted instructions and eventual sighs of relief. Rolled on its belly across the room and up a ramp, the *talha* was temporarily repositioned so it could be tipped on its head over a set of blocks, under which a roaring fire would be built.

After everyone caught their breath, it was all backs and shoulders into it again, accompanied by sounds of seriously strained lifting. After a final collective shove upward, the *talha* was carefully shuffled into a fireable position. Well earned triumphant cheers followed. It was all quite reminiscent of that famous photo of the US Marines raising the American flag over Iwo Jima's Mount Suribachi. Iconic, but in different ways.

Thinking about what had just transpired, it was crystal clear the slightest slip or misstep at any point up to then could have ended in crushed bodies and broken bones.

Meanwhile the *pés* master had filled his pot with his special secret formula (beeswax, pine sap plus ???) and began heating this up in a cauldron. He told me that each mix always involved an element of impromptu calibration based on the size and shape of each *talha*.

Two hours later, with the room cast in a smoky haze and the *talha* hot enough to soak up melted *pés*, the process was ready to reverse itself.

Heating the *pés*

Then suddenly, an unexpected glitch. Only five pairs of gloves were available. Meaning fewer men and relatively more weight to wrestle. What had been merely a dangerously heavy *talha* was now dangerously hot as well and a whole lot more hazardous. Nevertheless, there was no alternative but to get on with it. After considerably more shouting, staccato warnings, grunts and smoke-induced tears, eventual sighs of relief announced it was down on its belly again.

Hot Waxing

From there the *pés* master took over, ladling copious quantities of his boiling hot, blackened mixture into the *talha's* guts. The team rolled the *talha* around on its belly to cover as much of the inside as possible, leaving the lower third, where the 'mother' resides, uncoated. The *pés* master painted the interior with a broom-sized brush, eventually sealing the inside of the remaining belly, shoulder, neck and outer collar. The *pés* quickly hardened into a brownish, enamel-like gloss.

At that point everyone took a much needed break, tearful, coughing and desperate for a cold beer. After the smoke cleared and the *talha* cooled down a bit, they raised it back into its original position. The whole operation took about 4-5 hours. At that point I left for an 11 pm dinner and they all went back to tackle the evening's second *talha*; something that would hold their attention well into the early hours of the morning.

Shaking the *pés*, with much shouting, grunting and sweating

As I ate, safely, a classic plate of pork and clams, all I could think of was how many thousands of times *talha* had gone through this treatment in the past. And yet, it was only recently that enough *talha* were in use again to create a market demand large enough to keep an emerging group of professional *pés* masters in enough part-time seasonal work to keep them going. The process I had the privilege to watch now, a hundred years ago would have been an everyday occurrence on most streets of every village and town in Alentejo before harvest time. It simply boggled the mind.

To pés or not to pés? That is the question.

When I began my foray into *talha* culture a decade ago, *pés* was mysterious stuff. The handful of people I was talking to then had limited direct experience themselves and were mostly relaying second hand information they'd gleaned from older, mostly retired winemakers. Some of this was vague and, at times, contradictory and probably a lot of what I was hearing got lost in or left out of translation as well.

Much more is known about *pés* now than a few years ago. Historical information has come to light and a lot more practical knowledge has been rediscovered, through direct experience during the more recent revival period. The consensus now suggests the basic formula is a mixture of beeswax and pine sap, with or without olive oil and/or thyme or other aromatic herbs.

Previous testimony suggested *pés* was applied to reduce liquid leakage or reduce oxidation by filling in porous ceramic walls or for easier cleaning or simply to flavor the wine. All plausible, either individually or in combination. Several sources also indicated it was often possible in the past to taste a wine and identify the *pés* master involved, suggesting a professional hierarchy and a preference by some for what *pés* added to wine characters. Indeed, after a decade of tasting *talha* wine I'm much better at perceiving *pés's* influences than I was initially.

It's now clear there are several practical and historical reasons behind *pés*.

Going back over 6,000 years ago to the beginnings of terracotta winemaking in the mountainous regions straddling modern Georgia and Armenia, it is clear that pot makers have always had the option to glaze their pots, inside or out, making them as air and watertight as glass or modern stainless steel tanks. And yet all clay pot winemaking cultures since ancient times have consistently rejected creating an anaerobic (reductive) environment like this.

At some point someone must have tried wine from glazed and unglazed pots and recognized unglazed made much better wine, as in softer and more integrated. They may not have understood the scientific reasoning behind why, but clearly there was a preference for allowing micro amounts of oxygen to breathe through a pot's walls. Up until the recent rediscovery of terracotta winemaking, oak barrels performed a similar micro-oxygenation role in modern winemaking.

Creating and maintaining the optimal porosity of a *talha's* walls is central to terracotta winemaking. Although stopping liquid from leaking is also important, allowing just the right amount of oxygen to seep into the wine is much more important.

Finding the optimal rate of oxygen transference rate (OTR) is the key here. Letting in too much oxygen oxidizes the wine too quickly, whereas letting in too little will stunt a wine's development, making it unpleasantly raw, sharp and hard to drink during its first year of life - which is when most *talha* wine was drunk up in the past.

And which brings us back to *pés*. Pine resin, beeswax and olive oil all 'breathe' to greater or lesser extents. And all provide waterproof surfaces to varying degrees, making them ideal to perform both functions. It's the mix that becomes greater than its parts, boiling down to a magical combination of something that's just sticky, slick, hard, waterproof and spicy enough, without being too much.

Following ancient practices, Georgian *qvevri* pots receive only a single internal coating of beeswax. This is applied when the pots are fresh from the kiln and still piping hot, so the wax is instantly sucked up and deeply absorbed into the wall's pores. Although the pots are scrubbed clean yearly and wax eventually wears thin, it isn't reapplied.

Several Georgian winemakers indicated a single waxing was enough to waterproof them against ground water seeping in or wine seeping out after burial. That said, other winemakers chose to apply whitewash or concrete to the outside of their pots to avoid seepage. Apparently groundwater and/or the soils they were buried in played in to this practice.

But I was also told by two master pot makers that if *qvevri* are made with the right combination of clays and fired correctly, the pots shouldn't leak. They indicated that the addition of beeswax was there to fill in the clay more uniformly and create a clean surface. Being buried the earth probably inhibits oxygen transference to a greater degree than for freestanding *talha*.

The major difference between the two pots is that *talhas* sit above ground, directly connected to the atmosphere. External evaporation and temperatures may influence why *pés* is reapplied over time and why pine resin, olive oil and other ingredients were chosen over and above *qvevris'* simple beeswax treatment. Depending on the ratios of components, *pés* develop a relatively hardened surface, somewhere between varnish and a thick epoxy. The more resin, the harder and denser it becomes.

Which brings us back to oxygen regulation. The reason why fine winemaking in the modern era is based around oak barrel fermentation and maturation is that oak lets in a tiny amount of oxygen that creates complexity: developing and integrating textures, aromas and flavors, while softening and refining tannins through polymerization. Terracotta pot winemaking can do as much, but at rates that are around two to four times faster than barrels. Several *talha* winemakers see this controlled oxidation as *talha's* greatest asset.

Some producers like Jose de Sousa, Herdade do Rocim, Susana Esteban, Fitapreta, Esporao…have consciously rejected *pés* applications. That said, all use 100-200-year-old *talha* that technically shouldn't need new *pés* to inhibit oxygen transference. The build up of *pés* and tartaric acid residue over time will have filled up the pores in the walls of their *talhas* many decades ago, regularizing oxygen transfer rates.

These producers also reject *pés's* intrusive flavors and aromas, preferring pure clay's neutrality; the same reasoning that drives the global 'amphora' wine movement.

So this is the great dividing line between those that do and those that don't. Interestingly, *pés* isn't required in the DOC regulations, so it remains discretionary.

Those that do use *pés* either like the spice and flavor it imparts to wine, or are intent on preserving the traditional practices that have been handed down. The former is in keeping with Greek, Roman and other ancient culture's practices where some of *pés's* ingredients - and more - were added to enhance wine characters.

Although adding non-grape 'additives' is the antithesis of modern winemaking's penchant for fruit clarity, it clearly was a prized practice in the past. Whether *pés* in *talha* wine continued from Roman or earlier times or was a spontaneous later development, remains to be clarified.

Of course, pine resin is still added to retsina wine in Greece. Although initially it can be shockingly turpentine-ish to modern tastebuds, after a couple of weeks of regular drinking it tends to become a pleasant, quintessential background character of that wine style. At least that's my experience. Similarly, freshly applied beeswax can leave telltale spicy, honeycomb-like characteristics in wine that eventually blend into the background of youngish *talha* wine.

Honorado's *pesgador* is from Pedro do Corval, historically one of the greatest centers of *talha* pot production in previous centuries. His formula follows a mixture of rosemary, lavender and other herbs from local fields mixed with honey, beeswax and pine resin.

As mentioned earlier, Professor Ruivo remembered *pés* as a mix of rosemary, thyme, pine-nut tree resin and olive oil, boiled together so it 'wasn't too liquid or too solid' and the resin characters didn't dominate the wine. Antonio Gato recalled that the *talhas* were scrubbed with fennel before recoating. One can imagine that, and/or many other local herbs like oregano, sage… may have been added to spice up preferential *pés* concoction.

Outeiros Altos's winemaker Virgilio Rodrigues heard from oldtimers that there were many *pés* variations in his subregion near Estremoz. By the time he began using *talha* the whole tradition had vanished. The best formula he could piece together from older locals was that pine resin and beeswax were constants, with local herbs the variable. Lacking any specific ratios he is still working this out through ongoing experimentation.

For him the most important thing is to avoid intrusive burned, smoky, charcoal-like aromas. He dislikes how these intrude on his carefully grown grapes' characters. Avoiding overheating in kettles he heats *pés* gently up to a melting point and then applies this directly to the *talha* walls using a blow torch. OK, maybe not traditional, but it is clearly a way of fine-tuning *pés* to get exactly what his wines want from it.

Another question that is still being answered is how long does a coat of *pés* last? There are patches of residues evident inside 400+ year old *talha*, so the short answer is a long time. On a more experiential level, where winemakers taste the wines on a regular basis, directly sensing the ongoing influence of *pés* on wine, timings for reapplication varied. Generally the answer was along the lines of 'when it needs it' suggesting more instinct and art, than science, is at play. Others, like Quinta da Picarca, told us they recoat their *talha* around every eight years or so. When I suggested that time frame to other winemakers I got back a that's-about-right kind of nod.

What's currently interesting about this is that although today's *talha* winemakers have been given many hints about how wines were made in the past, there is still much to be rediscovered through ongoing hands-on experience and experimentation. It's all very much a living art, still in the process of rediscovering itself. *Pés* is one small part of that.

And a little olive oil for good measure

It may seem odd to many of us, but before corks were used, olive oil was the chosen way to preserve wine from oxidizing. Indeed the world's oldest bottle of wine, housed in Germany's Pfalz Historical Museum, was sealed with a layer of olive oil 2000 years ago and continues to preserve the wine below.

A *talha* has two things against it in terms of quick oxidation. The wine's upper surface, where it is exposed to air, is very large and ever changing. During its first couple of months, when filled to the brim, the new wine is traditionally covered with wooden or terracotta plugs, thus eliminating direct exposure to air. The problem comes after tapping in November. Thereafter glasses and pitchers of wine are drawn from the bottom and the upper surface steadily drops, changing its location and size daily, exposing the wine's surface to increasingly larger amounts of oxygen.

The simple historical solution has been to pour olive oil across the top, creating a barrier that adapts to these changes, continually covering the entire surface from wall to wall until the *talha* is empty.

A decade ago, the main objections I heard to this old practice was that oil would mix into the last upper level of the wine and ruin it. Another concern was that oil would soak into the *talha's* walls, polluting any wine made in it later and ruining the pot forever.

Most of these concerns have proved groundless. Modern power washers and other forms of cleaning are able to clean and renew pots yearly. In terms of drainage, it's only the last few pitchers of wine that capture any of the residual oil. If anything, this provides a warning that it is time to move on and tap the next *talha*.

Another early complaint was that the cover of oil made it very difficult to clear a large enough space to dip a glass in from the top to collect samples to check a young wine's development. Indeed, I observed oil being repeatedly shoved out of place before dipping, only to see the oil slip right back into its original position. It was a problem clearly needing a solution.

And then a simple one appeared. On my last trip someone (maybe the people from Pais das Uvas or XXVI Talha) had miraculously rediscovered an ancient solution. By gently blowing across the surface the oil suddenly withdrew in ripples, leaving a gaping place to dip freely.

A case of a new dog, old tricks or old dog, new tricks, who knows?

Fact is, it works like a charm.

Chapter Six
Talha at the Center of Village Life

It's difficult for us in the 21st century to understand how central *talha* were to village life in Alentejo, nor how *talhas'* decline contributed to the depopulation of the region over time.

Historically, the relatively isolated greater Vidigueira region, including Cuba, Alvito, Vila de Frades, Vila Alva and Vidigueira, would have been some of the most impoverished parts of Portugal, a country, which up until the end of the 20th century was one of the poorest in Europe. Blazingly hot, dry and dusty in summer, life was hard.

Alentejo has long been a land of proud and hard-working people, nevertheless, life there never would have been easy. Village life would have been relatively unchanged from Roman times. Large, quasi-feudal landowners controlled most of the countryside, with villages cropping up within walking distance to supply people to work the land and provide other services. Village families would have supplemented meagre incomes with subsistence gardening and perhaps a few vines of their own on tiny plots on the edge of town. Bartering and sharing and people watching out for each other would have been the only insurance coverage for bad times..

In many ways greater Vidigueira was a place forgotten by time. Many of these villages weren't electrified until late in the 20th century, with the economic and daily life not unlike rural America during the depression era of the 1930s, say Texas or Tennessee. With no internet, television, cinema, concert halls or even radio for distraction, each village's small *tascas* and larger *tabernas* remained the heart and soul of the community.

They served a community function not unlike pubs have done in the UK; providing heated rooms in winter where people could pop in for a quick drink or bite to eat, chat, catch up on gossip and after a few glasses, break out into Alentejo's uniquely indigenous form of polyphonic song. Most importantly, they were centers of power and information, where men gathered after work and discussed politics, farming techniques or crop prices.

When I first started exploring *talha* back in 2012, it seemed as if very little of *talha* culture had survived. I visited a handful of adegas and knew of Gato's *tasca* which was on its last legs and now closed, plus two other large, *taberna*-type restaurants: Pais das Uvas and Cuba's Monte Pedral.

What I hadn't realized was there was a hidden part of *talha* culture that was still alive in villages. This was much more privately protected and simply wasn't being shared with me yet. I had to earn the right of entry.

But there were other things going on as well. The Portuguese are notoriously shy and modest. I'm sure some were fearful I might see some of this as too backward, rather than the wonderful charm I definitely would have seen.

Some older Portuguese can suffer from a stubborn streak of unneighborliness, believing my wine and village is best and my neighbor's is always worse. I recall a local singer performing a traditional 'ultra-local' folk song about a villager singing to his neighbor about his village. It went something like… 'my village may be a dusty, desolate, stinking hot, falling apart pile of bricks, but at least it's not as bad as yours.' Tongue in cheek, self deprecating humor of course, but also a touch true.

And so it was to my utter shock that after having repeatedly visited Cuba, Vila de Frades, Vidigueira and other *talha* centers over the years, I finally made it to Vila Alva, just another five clicks down the road from Vila de Frades.

It was a revelation. Easily missed, off to the side of a narrow secondary road, it was a tiny place with only 400 residents. There may have been a cafe or takeaway tucked away somewhere, but the best place to eat was in the community center, where delicious homemade grub was served up by a couple of grandmotherly types at dirt cheap, people's prices. Clearly not large enough for a supermarket, the village might have had a tiny hole-in-the-wall shop for basic supplies. Although it was clean and tidy and nicely painted up, Vila Alva clearly had seen better days.

I was there to visit the young team at XXVI Talhas as they sealed their largest *talha* with *pés* for the first time. I had tried their wines in 2019, liked them, and knew the story of how a group of four childhood friends, born and raised in Vila Alva, were re-establishing their grandfather's winery Adega Mestre Daniel. Basically they had unlocked the doors of the old adega - mothballed since 1985 - found 26 intact *talhas* inside, scrubbed them up and now they were making great wine again.

But there was another level of intent going beyond just revitalizing the family's old *talha* winemaking business. All were deeply committed to resurrecting their little village's fortunes, which has been haemorrhaging a hundred people every decade for years.

During a break watching the high drama of *pés* application at XXVI Talha, one of their young friends invited me to have a look at his future project half a block up the road. After unlocking a large door, inside stood another twenty large *talhas* standing, dust covered and unused, 'involuntarily mothballed' just as Adega Mestre Daniel's had been.

XXVI Talha's plan was infectious. Chatting with Daniel Parreira I asked if more mothballed adegas were hidden around the village. His response floored me. There were at least eight adegas with over 130 *talhas*, STILL producing wine in Vila Alva at that point. Another fourteen adegas were mothballed behind locked doors containing over 86 unused *talhas*. He reckoned all could return to production relatively quickly. This, of course, compares with the hundreds more that existed pre-20th century, when vineyard totals steadily shrank from 1200 down to present 400 hectares.

Daniel Parreira and his cousin João Taborda have produced a beautifully researched booklet, "Vila Alva - Terras de Vinho," 2018, as part of an exhibition they created to celebrate Vila Alva's *talha* culture.

The booklet documents grape and *talha* wine production going back to Roman occupation through the 21st century and previously unknown local *talha* fabrication, alongside the broader aspects of how central *talha* culture was to the daily life of the village.

It boggles the mind that in 1950 Vila Alva had reached its peak of 1300 people with over 70 small and medium sized wineries - one for every 18 people! In addition, almost every household had a small *talha* (*tareco*) opened on St. Martin's Day, that supplied family needs through to the next vintage. Those were happy times when people could pop into a neighborhood *tasca*, *taberna*, restaurant or adega, have a quick glass and fill up a jug to take home for family dinner.

But it's coming back...

During 2021's St. Martin's Day celebrations I finally made my way into the inner sanctums of village *talha* culture. The crew at XXVI Talha took me on a *tasca* crawl. The first stop was a young winemaker, ensconced in his family's garage sized basement, where we tasted his newly minted red and whites from 600 liter *talha*. Down the road more doors were flung open and filled glasses were offered up for an opinion.

And then on to an older well established, subterranean *taberna*. There was no sign outside an anonymous door. Clearly, only locals knew what it offered. The room was large, with space for five or six tables full of locals and a dozen large *talha*, the oldest from 1680. There was an open fire in one corner keeping the atmosphere cozy and meat roasted on grills.

After we had a couple of glasses, freshly drained from the *talha's* bottom, the atmosphere relaxed and we were made to feel at home. People offered us chairs at their table and cheerfully pro-offered food off their platters. More people entered with slabs of uncooked meat and slapped these on the grill.

Then it dawned on me. The only thing for sale here was wine, everything else on offer was free and meant to keep customers warm, happy and comfortable, so they would keep coming back for more wine. This was a place where profits were of secondary concern. It was a place for people in the community to gather and enjoy each other's company.

Vila Alva is not alone. There is clearly a sea change gathering around *talha*.

The same pattern of reclamation and innovative rebirth can be seen across Alentejo with 20-30 somethings carrying on where their tired parents and retired grandparents have left off. Professor Arlindo's grand-daughter Teresa has revitalised his old adega, newly renamed Gerações da Talha. The sons of venerable *talha* restaurateurs at Pais das

St. Martin's Day *talha* crawl...

Uvas have refurbished a ruined 17th century adega next door, to bottle their new Honrado-branded DOC wines. Rui Reguenga has fought a long hard battle to restore Portalegre's *talha* heritage and their associated old vineyards. The dynamic couple of 40 somethings at Herdade do Rocim have promoted *talha* globally, and welcome the world to come visit and enjoy the experience firsthand for themselves.

New restaurants and hotels and Airbnbs have opened, supported by new artisanal products. Villages have scrubbed up and are looking good again.

The future looks bright, and all because of *talha*.

Chapter Seven
Talha's Traditional Grape Varieties

The first time I tasted Alentejo's *talha* wines I was struck by how different they were from anything I'd tasted before. Compared to the modern-styled production wines I had previously tasted from Alentejo - which were easily mistaken for Australian or Californian wine styles - *talha* wine tasted more of the grapes they were made from, were less fruity and aromatic, usually much lower in alcohol and higher in acidity. They could only have been from Alentejo.

On the other hand, they were also very different from other, traditionally-made, clay pot, *qvevri*-made wines I'd experienced from Georgia. *Talha* wines were lighter and fresher and fruitier and less alcoholic, nothing like the heavier, more astringent *qvevri* wines, often called 'orange' wines because of the strong tannins and color they pick up from eight months of skin contact. *Talha* wines had a bit of 'skin' influence, but it didn't dominate characters.

Nor were they much like wines from the modern 'amphora' wine movement, which often leaned toward 'orange' wines or the vaguer category of 'natural' wine. Although *talha* certainly are born of natural fermentation, avoid chemical additions and sulphur preservatives, they are determined by their own traditions and technology, not an ideology or fashion.

Talha wines were clearly from a place following a traditional style honed over time. Their specialness comes down to their grapes, where they were grown, and how they are shaped by the pots that made them into wine.

What makes *talha* wines different?

The first big surprise was that almost all *talha* wines were white. That was clearly the tradition and that's what most of the locals preferred to drink. Later on I would learn that reds may have been a later commercial development that followed a market demand from outside the region.

Retired Professor Virgílio Loureiro offered an intriguing theory as to why, making a compelling case that this tradition is underpinned by religious practice. He reckons the church had a monopoly on red wine for sacramental purposes, and the peasants were left with white grapes to drink every day.

His research suggested that medieval Cistercian monks had exclusive rights to 'tint' wine. This entailed adding specially macerated, highly concentrated, extra dark red wine to white wine to match the color of blood for sacrament - hence the Iberian terms for red wine, tinto/ tinta. No one was allowed to drink red wines, which were called 'black wines' and considered the wine of the devil. The only safe option for common people was to make and drink white wine.

A similar religious association was echoed in Georgia - a deeply Christian culture - where 80% of *qvevri* wines are white. I was told by several producers that reds were traditionally considered 'black wines' and following devilish practices in recent times, they made sweet reds to sell to the Russian/Soviet market.

The second big surprise was how low the alcohol and high the acidity was in white *talha* wines. This, apparently, was due to a micro climate unique to the Vidigueira escarpment, which opens to cool, rainy weather from the Atlantic and protects the region from the hot winds off the Sahara Desert and eastern Spain.

But these characters also clearly have to do with the grape varieties in *talha* blends. Difficult to prove, but one has a sense that *talha* and *talha* grapes have a long, long evolutionary relationship together. Which suggests more questions! Did the grapes attract *talha* or the other way around? Were the typical blend of grapes developed to suit *talha* production or did *talha* luckily stumble on to a bunch of grapes that happened to be perfectly suited to clay pot fermentation? Most likely it's a bit of everything.

The uniqueness of Iberian grapes

There is much more to *talha* grapes than meets the eye. It turns out that Iberian wine grapes are quite different from the rest of Europe's grapes.

Up until the last decade or so, the prevailing scientific belief was that European wild grapes became extinct after having been scraped from the landscape during the last ice age that ended around 11,000 years ago. Grapes didn't appear again until they were domesticated by the ancient culture straddling modern Armenia and Georgia, where organized large-scale winemaking began around 6000-8000 years ago. Thereafter, those eastern grapes were distributed westward around the Mediterranean successively by the Phoenicians, Greeks and Romans through trade and conquest.

The implied assumption was that Iberian grapes and Iberian winemaking appeared late in European history.

We know now from DNA studies that this scenario was incorrect. Some of the original wild European grapes that predated the last ice age did, in fact, survive during summer melts within parts of southern Europe, especially the interior and coastlines of the Iberian Peninsula, and most especially in Portugal's Alentejo.

See: https://www.winedisclosures.com/endangered-grapes and https://www.vinetowinecircle.com/genetica/reflexoes-acerca-da-presenca-de-vitis-silvestris-na-iberia-urante-a-era-glaciar/

Many modern Iberian grapes still retain the DNA signatures of those most ancient European grapes, marking them out from the grapes arriving during later periods from the eastern Georgian/Armenian area.

All of this raises a lot of questions. Were some of the Portuguese grapes with distinct DNA originally domesticated from ancient, local wild grapes by Alentejo's indigenous Tartessian tribes and possibly earlier tribes? Might some also have cross-bred more broadly with other ancient Iberian grapes before the eastern grapes arrived? And what others may have cross-bred with later arrivals after the Tartessians and their remnants traded with outsiders like the Phoenicians after 9th century BC, Greeks (7th century BC), Romans (1st-4th century), Moors from Africa (9th-12th centuries), monks from Northern Europe (7th through 15th century and beyond) or other arrivals later still in the 19th and 20th centuries?

Drawing from several authors, University of Lisbon's Dr. Mkrtich Harutyunyan, summarizes what's known so far: 'It is believed that the Tartessians were the first to cultivate grapes on the Iberian Peninsula dating back to around 2000 BC, followed by the Iron Age Phoenicians, who took over the Tartessian trade.'

López-Ruiz and Pérez, (2016) shed further light on this (my italics): '...it is worth mentioning that, like in the case of mining, here the *Phoenicians introduced new techniques to maximize the production of resources that existed in wild form or were primitively cultivated in the area.* Current studies of the vine's genome and its relationship to the domestication of local variants, as well as archaeometric and stylistic analysis of materials involved in wine transportation and consumption, unequivocally support the crucial role of the Phoenicians in their introduction of wine and wine culture in the central and western Mediterranean, including Italy and Iberia.'

Amplifying this they also suggest 'deliberate merging of eastern variants of the plant with the local wild varieties, refining the local product through genetic as well as technological means.'

All of this indicates that Alentejo's Tartessians had an established wine culture of their own worth refining when the Phoenicians began to trade with them.

Still other research (Lavrador da Silva, Fernão-Pires, Bianchi-de-Aguiar, 2018) pushes organized grape-growing locally at least as far back as the Bronze and early Iron ages. 'The culture of vineyard cultures dates back at least 6000 years, with signs of plantations around 2000 years B.C.'

A good synopsis of the ancient Iberian wine history can be found on: https://www.vinetowinecircle.com/historia/idade-bronze-iber/ and https://www.vinetowinecircle.com/en/history/the-time-of-the-roman-empire/

There is still much left to unravel in all this, but it's pretty clear that winemaking and grape-growing, in some form or other, existed long before eastern cultures brought their own refined versions of wine production to Alentejo, possibly all the way back to when local hunters and gatherers first realized the basket of wild grapes they'd picked a few days earlier had been transformed into a magical drink.

Unraveling the layers

DNA studies are already hinting at possible local points of origination for Alentejo's grape varieties, as well as where others are more likely to have come from outside the area.

One important marker for where a grape variety may have originated is how diverse its local clonal material is compared to elsewhere. If a grape variety retains dozens or hundreds of local clonal variations, it is likely to have inhabited that place for a long time and mutated freely, compared to a vine brought in later, where all the vines are of a single clonal type.

An excellent example of this is Antão Vaz. This grape was barely known outside of Alentejo until a few years ago, where its genetic diversity remains very high throughout the region. Tellingly, some of Antão Vaz's highest concentrations of diversity are captured in old vineyards owned by members of the Adega Cooperativa da Vidigueira, Cuba e Alvito and Vitifrades.

I spent time with its general manager, José Miguel Almeida, visiting one of the oldest, most interesting of its vineyards. It was clearly very old; at least 130+ years old, possibly even older. Planted, ungrafted on its own roots, it possibly predates the phylloxera epidemic, protected from the phylloxera louse by the loose sandy soil the vines grow in. The gnarly old vines there are unexpectedly bonsai-like, tiny and thin-limbed, clearly stunted from long lives within a challenging - read hostile - growing environment: drought prone, infertile, hot as hell...

Old vines at Cooperativa Vidigueira

The viticulture is of an ancient type, extremely rare even amongst old vines: rowless, interspersed by olive trees and planted helter skelter in low-to-the-ground bush vine, goblet configurations. The vineyard looked as if it had gone completely feral with vines, haphazardly peppering the landscape. Some growing inches apart, others with meters between. It was a vineyard more about individual plants than a cohesive band of varietals. At least thirty different varieties were interplanted with rarely a single adjacent match up to be seen anywhere.

Almeida said several of the vines remain unknown awaiting analysis; if lucky, it would earn its very own new name or, if not, at least some relational association to an existing variety. Clonal variation was extremely high amongst many of the identifiable vines, indeed, some the highest found anywhere in Portugal.

The vineyard suggested a possible point of origination for several of the varieties where parent, grandparent and great-grandparent vines had been replanted *in situ* over centuries. The ultimate in intensive farming. Although some DNA work had been completed, much more was needed to complete the picture.

São Cucufate is a relatively short walk away. That begged the question, did this vineyard contain the residue of vines that once grew at São Cucufate 2000 years ago? Possibly earlier?

And yet, this was only one of many 100+ year old vineyards that the cooperative still farms and makes wines from. There are many pockets of old vines like these that time forgot; an amazing abundance of biodiversity found nowhere else. Perhaps Alentejo's greatest hidden asset; most certainly its collective intellectual property going back generations…

Talha's grapes

These vineyards also record a common mixture of grapes that was closely allied to *talha* winemaking; perhaps going back 50, 100, 1000 or more years? Their luck in surviving has a lot to do with the nature of cooperatives. The rule is to take whatever grapes their members bring in. After owners shifted from *talha* to cooperative production, they simply carried on growing and gathering the same grapes they always had for *talha*, except now they were absorbed into the cooperative's massive production. Lost in space, so to speak.

Fortunately the cooperative applied no pressure to grub them up, replant with more commercially oriented, more fashionable single varieties and string them up in rows on modern trellis systems, irrigate and pick them with machines. Happily, these traditional grapes remained firmly planted in the ground where they had comfortably lived for over a century, possibly many centuries.

The nature of *talha's* old field blend vineyards

Alentejo, like most of Portugal, has a long tradition of blended wines rather than single grape varietal bottlings. Traditionally vineyards mixed up to 30-40 different grape varieties in 'field blends' that effectively grew the final grape assemblage in the vineyard, then purposefully harvested them together at the same time and co-fermented the lot in a single mass. All this is quite the opposite of modern practices where grapes are fermented separately and then assembled in desired proportions to make a final stylistic blend.

These old, mixed, field blend vineyards endured much longer and have survived in larger numbers in Alentejo than in most other parts of Portugal or the rest of the world for that matter. As such they provide a window into what the most typical blends of grapes going into *talha* wine were during the last century and, possibly, centuries past.

The Hidden Sense of Alentejo's Mixed Variety, Old Vineyards

Old vines, apart from preserving biodiversity, are incredible assets on many other levels. Normally most vines are ripped out at forty years of age because their juice production drops per plant, making them less profitable. However, the positive side of that is the juice is more concentrated, complex and higher quality. Less really is better.

This is simply due to reproductive necessity. Old vines compete by creating fewer, but sweeter berries that attract hungry birds which eventually carry their seeds off into new territories.

Recent scientific studies have demonstrated other advantages. Older vines are less disease prone and more drought resistant (having repeatedly survived the worst of them). They need less water because their roots have grown deep over the years sourcing consistent water supplies. Stacking it all up, they require less work, fewer resources and yet still produce better wine.

Similarly, the older traditional practice of mixing different grapes into the same vineyard is increasingly recognized for its own inherent qualities. Until the last decade or so, mixed vineyards were frowned on in some parts of Portugal as representing a stubborn adherence to an embarrassing old-fashioned way of doing things. Clearly primitive, it represented something from the realm of unsophisticated peasant farming, something needing to be moved beyond. Not unlike previous views about *talha* wine culture, everything about mixed-vine vineyards represented the antithesis of scientifically-driven modern winemaking and viticulture.

And yet, from the beginning of time up until the middle of the last century, growing multiple grape varieties in the same vineyard at the same time was not only common throughout the world, but made the most farming sense.

From that perspective, it was a simple way of hedging one's bets - natural crop insurance. Growing twenty or more varieties together in one spot, year in, year out, would ensure at least some of the vines produced good enough fruit to harvest. In good years, a lot of good wine was produced. In rainy seasons or drought-ridden years, there was at least some wine to drink.

The modern criticism for this practice is that multiple grape vineyards don't deliver uniform ripening, nor provide a single focused flavor profile. And so old mixed-vine vineyards have been on a downward spiral toward extinction for decades.

In a world obsessed with divas, they prefer to sing more harmoniously within the anonymity of a choir.

But perceptions have changed in some quarters, and old mixed-vine vineyards have taken on a special status globally. The concentration factor created by age is increasingly obvious in the final wines. Co-fermenting many varieties also creates its own complexity in terms of flavor, aromas, texture and structure. The wines are often seen to be more thoroughly married together when co-fermented, compared to those assembled from parts after fermentation.

Secondly, there is now an awareness that weeding out dead vines over the course of a century creates a more cohesive crop. Whereas in its young days a vineyard might have had a three-week ripening period between its ripest and most unripe grapes, after years of replacing dead vines with ones that thrived inside a vineyard, that ripening window might be reduced to within a week. Like the advantage older vines bring, mixed vines become super-adapted to their vineyard, making them more resilient and productive.

Human intervention and natural adaptation have created a unique terroir statement where vines are expressing plants perfectly suited to a piece of ground after having thrived there for so long.

The Grapes that go into *Talha's* Subregional Blends

Rather than include all the grapes currently allowed in Alentejo wines, the focus below is on the grapes most traditionally associated with *talha* winemaking. These differ from subregion to subregion, following what winemakers found most suited to their local climate and soils and the style of wines they preferred to drink. Although all the grapes discussed below might crop up anywhere in Alentejo, each subregion tends to have local favorites in their basic blend.

The greater Vidigueira region retains the most intact *talha* culture and includes many historic vineyards around Saõ Cucufate, Vidigueira, Vila de Frades, Cuba, Alvito and Vila Alva. The region is famous for its unexpectedly cool micro-climate, especially sympathetic to white blends made from Antão Vaz, Roupeiro, Rabo de Ovelha, Perrum, Diagalves, Larião and Mantuedo. Although less important and smaller in output, the red blends tend to mix Trincadeira, Moreto, Tinta Grossa and Aragonez.

To the east and much warmer, Reguengos de Monsaraz favors red blends from Grand Noir, Moreto and Tinta Grossa. White output, because of the heat, is much smaller and less important. It essentially shares Vidigueira's blend, while adding the near extinct variety Sarigo.

Further east bordering Spain and hotter still, Granja-Amareleja has the highest concentrations of the red Moreto grape, which is commonly blended with Tinta Grossa and Trincadeira. Whites follow Vidigueira's mixture; according to Professor Virgilio Loureiro. Roupeiro is prized for its special honeyed aromas (called 'toasty' notes by locals); Perrum (offering structure, tannin, and acidity); and Rabo de Ovelha, for quantity.

To the north, covering a higher, cooler plateau, reds dominate Borba's output, tending toward Trincadeira, Castelão and Alicante Bouschet with whites containing Rabo de Ovelha, Roupeiro, Tamarez. Similarly situated, Estremoz reds traditionally tend more towards Aragonez, Alfrocheiro and Trincadeira.

Mountainous Portalegre and vineyards close to nearby Roman ruin at Ammaia favor *talha* whites made up of Roupeiro and the Vidigueira mix, sometimes adding northern grapes, Arinto and Bical. Older red vineyards contain Trincadeira, Moreto, Castelão, Aragonez, along with other traditional Dao-Douro varieties: Tinta Carvalha, Alfrocheiro, Corropio, and Tinta Francesa.

The White Grapes

A note of special thanks to the renowned Armenian grapevine geneticists and bio-archaeologist, Dr. Nelli Hovhannisyan, for her help unraveling the mysteries of grape DNA below.

Antão Vaz

This grape is most certainly Alentejo's most important white variety and is thought to have originated in Vidigueira, where its oldest vines continue to grow and show the greatest genetic diversity (see Vidigueira Cooperativa). Antão Vaz wasn't known much outside of Alentejo and really only started migrating into parts beyond with the advent of modern refrigerated stainless steel tanks in 1980/90s. It was very much a forgotten grape.

Antão Vaz tends to be the dominant white grape in *talha* blends adding (subtle tropical) fruit, texture, balanced acidity and moderate alcohol 12.5%. A solid all rounder, it makes a good base around which other grapes can extend acidity or add their own characters, minerality, aromatics, etc. to the mix. Its thick skins resist sunburn, also offering oxidation-resistant tannins ideal to counter *talha's* oxidative fermentation. From a grape growing perspective, it is relatively robust in drought conditions, consistently producing good crops of balanced wines.

The grape's downsides are it can suddenly over-ripen, becoming heavy and thick, quickly losing acidity. Countering this, the trend with many younger *talha* winemakers is to pick early at 12%, to capture herbal & blossom-like florals and tart lemony acidity. In genetic terms, its parents are Joao Domingos and Sarigo/Cayetana Blanca (Hebén grandparent).

Roupeiro (Siria)

Roupeiro is an old grape first mentioned in the early 16th century and probably originating much earlier given how ubiquitous it is throughout southwestern Spain and Portugal's interior, ranging from Trás-os-Montes down to the Algarve. It was first mentioned in 1531 in Dao where it's called Siria, and may have originated inland near Guarda, given its clonal diversity there.

It produces good volumes with moderate alcohol and acidity. A late ripening grape, it likes warmer climates, so works well in Alentejo. Generally it is known for its strong aromatic and fruit profile, but my experience of Alentejo suggests a more fundamental mineral character, while just hinting at blossom-like florals, dried herb and spice aromas. Fruit characters range between melons, citrus and apples. Relative to most other grapes of the *talha* blend, it is the most aromatic and fruity of the lot. Esporaõ produces an excellent 100% Roupeiro *talha* wine from ungrafted old vines. DNA indicates its parents are Hebén-Fogasao (grandparent Savagnin Blanc) and Savagnin, suggesting deeper French-Iberian ancestry.

Perrum (Pedro Ximénez)

Perrum is more famously known as Pedro Ximénez in Spain's Jerez, for making intensely sweet, raisiny, fortified, dessert Sherries. Interestingly, it's never fulfilled that function within Alentejo's *talha* wines, where it only produces table wine and is harvested fresher, for a completely dry, lighter style.

Whereas Pedro Ximénez is marked by intensely sweet treacle, coffee, raisin fruit character that is crucially counterbalanced by high acidity keeping them from cloying, Perrum's early-harvested fermentation retains very high acidity with considerably fresher, fruitier, citrus characters.

It is commonly found amongst the old field blends grown in central and south eastern Alentejo, from Vidigueira through hotter Granja-Amareleja bordering Spain and up into cooler Portalegre. It is parented by Iberia's ubiquitous Hebén and another unknown, possibly extinct variety.

Mantuedo

Mantuedo, like Perrum and Diagalves, is commonly shared with neighboring western Andalucia, where it's called Listán de Huelva, a component of Fino Sherry. Interestingly, Huelva was a coastal center of Phoenician trade and the river it straddles flows up into central Alentejo.

There isn't a lot of available information on Mantuedo. Drought-resistant, thin-skinned and prolific, its main assets are high productivity and high alcohol, neutralish mineral characters, and lowish acidity. Often associated with Diagalves in blends. DNA suggests parentage by Mollar Cano (Hebén is grandparent) and an unknown grape.

Diagalves

Another thick-skinned, late-ripening grape perfectly suited to hot climates and *talha* winemaking, with skin tannins robust enough to counter *talha's* oxidative fermentation. It adds an interesting herbal aroma and volume, but not much else, as it is low in alcohol and acidity, needing support from more minerally, acidic grapes like Roupeiro and Perrum.

Diagalves's thick skins also make it ideal for *pendura* preservation as a table grape. Prof. Manuel Malfeito Ferreira mentions this dual purpose, fulfilling a role of 'traditional table grapes... the locals call them "pendura" grapes because they used to hang (pendurar) below the ceilings to store and keep eating over the year. So they have thick skins that endure "pendura". Some 40-50 years ago Amareleja was famous for its table grapes and locals continue to call them pendura, even if they no longer hang it.'

I first observed *pendura* when visiting Prof. Arlindo's winery (see photos Gerações da Talha) where CO2 collects during fermentation at ceiling level, preserving freshness differently than sun dried raisins. DNA indicates it is parented by Hebén-Alfrocheiro (Savagnin Blanc grandparent).

Larião

Locally called 'uva de algibeira,' suggesting Moorish origins or use during their occupation. Little is known about Larião. It's believed to be an old variety that's rarely found outside of old mixed vineyards and thought to be relatively endangered. DNA indicates a cross between Hebén and Almeur Bou Ahmeur grapes.

Sarigo (Cayetana Blanca)

This is another ancient, nearly extinct Alentejo grape, also called Cayetana Blanca in Spain where it originates. It has over 110 synonyms, suggesting, like Hebén, it has lived all over Iberia for a long time. Ironically, Sarigo is so ancient, rare and unknown that it isn't officially on the DOC grape registry. This has created problems for Jose de Sousa who isolated it in their old mixed vineyard and successfully produced *talha*-made wine from Sarigo but can't label it as Vinhos de Talha DOC because it isn't a sanctioned grape. Parented by Hebén and an unknown grape. Significantly, it parented Antão Vaz, Rabo de Ovelha and Tinta Grossa.

Rabo de Ovelha

Rabo de Ovelha has a similar grape bunch shape to a 'ewe's tail', hence its name. It's thought to have originated in Alentejo where it shows the highest clonal diversity. Highly productive, late ripening and thick-skinned, it does well in Alentejo's heat. It is not a predominant *talha* grape, more often showing up in small quantities as background material and component in old field blended vineyards. Parented by an unknown grape and Sarigo/Cayetana Blanca (Hebén grandparent).

Arinto

Arinto is a primary grape in Lisboa and Bairrada and probably not a mainstream, traditional *talha* variety. It does appear in old, mixed vineyard blends in Alentejo's cooler, elevated regions centered around Portalegre. Portugal's answer to Riesling, Arinto is marked by a pervasive minerality, spicy aromatics, tight, linear texture and searingly high acidity. Fruit characters tend toward the lemon-lime spectrum. A great structural wine that ages well. Parents are Hebén and Alfrocheiro (Savagnin Blanc grandparent).

The Red Grapes

Moreto

My first tasting of wine made from Moreto was a revelation. It made impressive wine which I liked a lot, but it made no sense. Produced from grapes grown in blazing hot Granja-Amareleja region - where it can bake in 45 degree C summers - I expected fire-breathing alcohol at blow-out levels above 15%, raisin-like flavors, flabby textures and desperately low acidity.

It was nothing like that. Instead it offered up pure red cherry juiciness, linear textures, refreshingly zippy acidity and lowish alcohols between 12%-13%. It reminded me of a more acidic version of Alfrocheiro, one of my favorite northern Portuguese grapes from Dao's cooler climate. Now it all makes more sense, as recent DNA research has determined that Moreto was grandparented by Alfrocheiro.

Professor Manuel Malfeito Ferreira's experience with Moreto dates back to 2009 when he first made *talha* wines at Granja-Amareleja's Cooperative. After 'tasting blind throughout the harvest, the best wines were those from Moreto.' Further discussions with the local winemaker Jose Piteira suggested the best of these grapes 'were Moreto "manso", meaning Moreto pied franc [and] not susceptible to phylloxera in gravelly soils. Moreto in more fertile soils and under excessive irrigation is not good.'

Continuing, he explains why it is so suitable for hotter climates, 'Moreto is a late ripening variety and in cooler years it may not even reach 12%-13%.' It's clearly a grape that thrives in hot, relatively hostile, infertile environments. He added that thanks to rediscovery of the potentials of these first wines, 'now Moreto, and other old varieties, are being revitalized around Alentejo.' Parented by Malvasia Fina (Heben x Alfrocheiro) and an unknown parent.

Tinta Grossa

Similar to Moreto, there is very little written about Tinta Grossa, both of which are mostly grown between Vidigueira and Granja-Amareleja. Both are siblings sharing Alfrocheiro and Hebén as parents. And although they aren't lookalikes, they share some similarities - Tinta Grossa reminds me of a slightly coarser younger brother. Both share cherryish/red fruit characters, but Tinta Grossa's seem more on the dried, super-ripe raisiny side. Texturally more linear, Moreto is generally lower in alcohol, more tightly acidic with finer tannins compared to Tinta Grossa's rounder, fuller body and slightly more rustic tannic profile. Whereas Moreto may be more widely planted in Granja-Amareleja, it is interesting that Vila Alva is surrounded by a high concentration of Tinta Grossa vines, which villagers have traditionally called 'our grape.' It is parented by Sarigo/Cayetana Blanca and Alfocheiro (Savagnin Blanc grandparent).

Trincadeira Preta

Trincadeira Preta (meaning black) is also called Tinta Amarela in northern regions. It is one of Portugal's more under-rated red grapes, difficult to grow and on the outer edges of late ripening. Later ripening is an advantage in warmer parts of Alentejo, but less so in elevated cooler or more northern sites.

It is generally considered an excellent blender, adding floral, spicy, aromatic complexity, blackberry, logan/mulberry fruit depth and finesse via lighter, finish tannins. When perfectly ripe and concentrated it can make a high quality standalone wine with longevity.

It's an old variety stretching throughout Douro, Dao, Lisboa, Tejo and Alentejo, and is thought to have originated north and inland of Lisboa. Dr. Nelli Hovhannisyan indicates the parentage is unknown. According to genetic data, there are genetic relationships with Ramisco and Sercial.

Grand Noir de la Calmette

Grand Noir de la Calmette was developed in 1855 by Frenchman Henri Bouschet near Montpellier. The grape is parented by Rioja's noble Graciano and Bouschet Petit. Along with Bouschet's other major creation, Alicante Bouschet, both grapes have found an adopted home in Alentejo where they make wines far better than they do anywhere in France.

Both grapes make inky black wine from black skins and naturally dark red juice bleeding out from red pulp, hence being prized as tinting wines. Significantly, both retain high acidity and handle Alentejo's sun and heat. Flavors are usually in the black fruit realm, blackberries mainly, and have longish-grained tannins and juicy fruits. Grand Noir can have a spicy, peppery edge to it. Jose de Sousa's Domingos Franco prefers it to Alicante Bouchet, which he finds has 'unpleasant cabbage-like characters'.

In terms of *talha* wine production, being relatively new comers into Alentejo, the two grapes haven't historically played a strong role in traditional blends. Grand Noir, being the exception, has been central to Jose de Sousa's *talha* production reaching at least back into the 1930s.

Aragonez (Tempranillo)

Aragonez is a high-quality grape that grows all over Spain and Portugal: Rioja, Ribera del Duero, Penedes, Douro, Dao and Alentejo's Portalegre. Grown in the right climates, it is renowned for its spicy aromatics, and mix of red and black fruit characters and balanced tannins and acidity. Its main disadvantages in hotter climates is a sensitivity to drought and early ripening, leading to over-ripeness, loss of acidity and excessive alcohol.

In terms of *talha* winemaking, it appears as part of the blend with Trincadeira in cooler, mountainous Portalegre and the other elevated northern Alentejo regions: Estremoz and Borba. Portalegre has a unique, possibly more ancient, form of Aragonez in many of its old mixed vineyards. This has smaller, more flavor-filled berries with lower production and more concentrated juice. Parented by Albillo Mayor (Heben x unknown) and Benedicto.

Alfrocheiro

Alfrocheiro sometimes appears as a minor component in *talha* blends in Alentejo's elevated northern regions. Its greater significance is that it fathered or grandfathered more common red *talha* grapes: Moreto, Tinta Grossa and

Castelão. It loves the cooler climate of Dao; in hotter climates it tends to become less focused, flabby, drops acidity and can blow up into unbalanced high alcohol. Its smart minerality, tart cherry fruit characters, linear profile and high acidity shine through its descendants, all of which are much better adapted to central Alentejo's heat.

The interesting thing with Alfrocheiro is that it is parented by Savagnin Blanc and an unknown cultivar. As Savignin Blanc originated in Jura, we have no idea where and when it came into Portugal from France. Perhaps via monasteries or aristocratic intermarriage or much earlier via Phoenicians, Greeks or Romans?

Castelão

This grape is most common in the coastal regions below Lisbon, Palmela, Setúbal and the adjacent western and northern parts of Alentejo. It is most often found in *talha* blends around Portalegre, Estremoz and Borba. Fruit characters are always in the red fruit realm reminiscent of cherries, red currants, red plums and strawberries. Nicely structured with firm acidity and rustic tannins it can age well. Like Tinta Grossa, it is parented by Sarigo/Cayetana Blanca and Alfrocheiro.

So what makes the *talha* grapes special?

What is interesting about most of the Vidigueira whites is they are exclusively Iberian, having a parent or grandparent relationship with Hebén grapes. Hebén is an ancient grape variety ubiquitous throughout Iberia and North Africa (known there as Gibi) where it has parented at least 60 varieties. It is unusual in that, unlike self-pollinating vinifera varieties, it produces only female flowers, not unlike wild grape female plants.

Although it shares a North African connection, it's unclear whether Hebén was brought to Iberia during the Moorish occupation or taken back there after. Or perhaps originally distributed further afield much earlier by the Phoenicians or even by migrating birds in deep antiquity.

The core white *talha* grapes with the purest Iberian ancestry are: Antão Vaz, Rabo de Ovelha, Perrum, Larião and Mantuedo. Although Roupeiro, Arinto and Diagalves share parentage via Hebén (or other Iberian grapes) they also contain French DNA via Savagnin Blanc, so they probably arrived later from further north. Regardless, taken together they still share a very strong Iberian ancestry and characteristics.

Aragonez is probably one of the oldest and most pure of the red Iberian grapes. Trincadeira's origins remain a mystery, but as a late ripener, it is well suited to both Alentejo and *talha*. Other later arriving reds Moreto, Tinta Grossa and Castelão parallel the half-breed nature of whites with Savagnin Blanc and Hebén ancestry.

One tiny puzzle piece in all this is Savagnin Blanc, given it remains a primary grape of France's Jura region. What's intriguing here is a possible association with the 6th century abbey of Saint-Pierre at Baume-les-Messieurs which is where Benedictine monks departed from to establish Cluny in Burgundy. It also has a long association with Benedictine and Cistercian monks who appear to have had connections with São Cucufate in the 1200s or possibly earlier.

Why these grapes became closely associated with *talha* is more difficult to answer. Probably most important is their ability to grow well in Alentejo's challenging hot climate and their abilities to make good wine in *talha's* oxidative environment. Grapes that are later ripening and drought resistant, with thick skins and high acidity, suit both parts of that equation. Which leaves other grapes, lacking some of these characteristics, to fill in gaps with their own distinct advantages: aroma, flavors, volume, alcohol, etc.

Who knows?

Old vines, young feet…the children of Vidigueira stomping the cooperative's century-old grapes

Chapter Eight
Potted History, Then and Now

Looking back a decade, it appeared that the secrets of *talha* pot production had died forever when the last master potters closed shop in the 1920s. No one knew anyone who had known anyone who had made *talha* pots. Nor were there any surviving records of the process nor any ruined kilns from the time to deconstruct how they might have been made. It all suggested replication was impossible.

All of the winemakers I spoke to then were using historic pots that they were lucky to have inherited, or scrounged from garden shops, antique stores or anywhere else they could be found. Everyone was fatalistically resolved to the likelihood that future *talha* wine production was forever limited to the 150 or so old pots that had survived.

After winning the battle to revive *talha* winemaking, the future growth of *talha* wine seemed self-limiting and headed towards an inevitable dead end.

But, like the arrival of the cavalry, over the last couple of years a massive number of lost *talha* pots have, quite literally, come out of the woodwork, many in shapes, forms and sizes previously unknown. Just as villagers in Vila Alva have begun opening long locked doors that had hidden away forgotten *talha*, other villages are unleashing their own treasure troves of old *talha* pots. A rough back of the napkin estimate suggests nearly 700 pots are in use now or awaiting refurbishment and return to production. Perhaps as many are still locked away and awaiting liberation.

Old *talha* with the makers mark

Alongside has been an explosion of information. Many *talha* are stamped with master's names, trademarks, production dates and places of manufacture. These easily contain enough data (going back to 1655) to flesh out a dandy PhD thesis focused on historical production. Many of these trademarks indicate multi-generations, indeed whole dynasties, of pot makers.

Historically, there were at least five major towns famous for *talha* pot production: São Pedro do Corval (formerly called Aldeia do Mato), Évora and Vila Alva in south central Alentejo with Campo Maior and Amieira do Tejo (Nisa municipality) based in the north. Of these, brands from Pedro do Corval and Campo Maior dominate surviving pots. Surprisingly, these towns didn't just service local markets. Many makers' pots were distributed widely across all regions, testifying to well-established reputations and a hierarchy of quality. This is no mean feat considering Campo Maior is a good 30-hour oxcart walk down to Vidigueira or 130km/80 miles as the crow flies.

From my first conversations with Jose de Sousa's Domingos Franco, it was clear that *talha* pots have their own special 'terroir'. After having worked wine in *talha* from all the major pottery centers, he had developed a clear preference for those made in nearby São Pedro do Corval. Unable to define exactly why, he reckoned they simply made better wine, to his taste anyway. Was this due to the clay, the way they were made, a strong manufacturing tradition, better kilns…all unanswerable questions for now? Incidentally, São Pedro do Corval remains a pottery town, barely surviving off tourists trinkets, terracotta plates, cups and garden statuettes.

The deeper question here is did pot-making develop in these centers because of proximity to special clay sources, or closeness to adegas and vineyards? What gravitated toward what and when?

How *talha* were made

After having observed Georgia's two greatest master *qvevri* makers first hand, it's clear that large scale pot making isn't rocket science. And it's also clear that there must have been similar techniques involved in producing large format *talha*. Both types of pots are of similar size, shape and thickness. For these reasons alone, modern *qvevri* pot production can tell us a lot about how *talha* pots were probably made in the past.

The only major differences are the holes at the bottom and that *talha* possibly may have needed to be a bit thicker and more robust because they have to stand alone, whereas *qvevri* are buried with walls reinforced by surrounding earth.

Giant 1200-1500 liter *qvevri* take about a month's worth of daily construction and drying time before final firing. *Qvevri* are built up from a short cone-shaped base that's been turned on a kick-wheel. Thereafter the remaining parts of the walls are hand-built atop this, with a new circular layer of clay about 2-3 inches high and thick, added each day. Each new layer is added by smashing a fat sausage-like tube of clay at 90 degree angles into the newly emerging wall. It requires a high degree of skill, involving a fairly quick and continuous slam-twist movement, accompanied by a simultaneous smoothing-out motion, perfectly coordinated with the second hand. It's quite a magical, transformational process to watch.

The kilns I observed in Georgia were of simple construction, about the size of a single car garage, made from bricks with a rounded, barrel-vaulted ceiling and a back wall with two holes at the top to let the smoke out. Each firing contains a half dozen large pots with wood packed tightly around each pot, leaving little empty internal space. The front door is bricked in last, leaving a small opening at the bottom to feed new firewood in during firing.

One truckload of wood is usually enough for firing. After the kiln is lit it burns for about a week, fed round the clock while the kiln master closely observes pots until they glow to a perfect red hot color, indicating optimal temperatures have been achieved. This is maintained for the right amount of time and eventually the fire is allowed to burn itself out. As mentioned earlier, beeswax is applied internally just after pots are removed while still hot, and rolled around to distribute wax evenly.

One *qvevri* maker explained how important the clay source was (a family secret) and that clay must be harvested at a precise time of year. He mentioned he sourced two different types of clay from the same riverbank, each dug out from different levels of strata, one more pliable and the other harder. The combination of the two was essential in creating strength and durability in the pot.

During our conversation he solved a mystery both Domingos Franco and I had pondered concerning one of Franco's exploded *talha*. A cross section showed a dark layer sandwiched between two lighter ones, which we had speculated may have indicated special clay combinations, an inner type sandwiched between the interior and exterior walls. In fact, the master said, this indicated a failed firing, it should have been uniformly colored throughout. A weakness that probably explained why the pot had exploded.

An exploded *talha* in Jose de Sousa's cellar

How old are *talha* pots, really?

Going back to my first encounters with *talha* culture, the assumption was that it was the last unbroken connection going back to Roman winemaking. Undoubtedly there is a lot of truth to this connection, but the more I delved into it, the more I noticed contradictions and gaps in this assumption. Lots of questions began arising. Was there more than met the eye? Perhaps our assumptions were wrong. Or at least not entirely right.

Could winemaking and grape-growing in Alentejo have gone back even earlier than the Romans? Were the Romans simply following on from a well established local wine culture, expanding and exploiting it further? What about the Phoenicians before them? Similarly, could the Phoenicians have simply connected into a pre-existing wine culture established by the local Tartessian tribes before them? Or did wine culture exist earlier still? Were the Portuguese being short changed?

Noticing the size and shape of surviving Roman *dolium*-like pots from São Cucufate and the ruined Roman city of Ammaia near Portalegre, these appeared to be much smaller, collarless and more heart shaped than later *talha*. After having encountered many pots from the 1600s through the 1920s, it suddenly dawned on me that there was a gaping hole of evidence from there back to Roman times.

Dolium from Roman Ammaia

Perhaps most significantly, *dolium* didn't appear to have *talha's* typical drainage holes in the bottom either. These holes are indicative of above ground fermentation and could have indicated an Alentejan innovation.

Of course the fact that only a tiny number of Portuguese-based *dolium* survived into modern times doesn't eliminate the possibility that many different shapes, sizes and types may have existed once, with or without lower holes. Still I couldn't help but wonder if the *talha* from the 17th to 20th centuries weren't a distinctive Portuguese development that had evolved far beyond their ancient antecedents?

In looking briefly for answers there wasn't anything immediately obvious or definitive from the few sources available then. Either these questions hadn't been asked or were still in the process of being researched and deciphered.

Fortunately I linked up with Dr. Mkrtich Harutyunyan, research scientist based at the University of Lisbon. As an Armenian - a region located in the northeastern part of the Armenian Highlands known as wine's 'Garden of Eden' - focused on how ancient wine and olive oil production spread around the Mediterranean Basin, he was perfectly positioned to direct me towards sources he has been researching.

Almost immediately, he passed on published evidence for holes in the bottom of pots found at Pompeii (Peña, 2007). Although holed pots didn't survive from São Cucufate and Ammaia, this at least proved they existed in Rome during Roman times.

Previous correspondence I had with one of ancient wine culture's foremost experts, Patrick McGovern, mentioned, 'I, too, was struck by the parallel with the *talhas*. My suspicion is that the practice and fermentation in jars above ground was introduced by the Phoenicians.'

Directing me to the 2019 second edition of his book, *Ancient Wine*, this mentions examples of pre-fired holes made near the base of 'Chalcolithic wine jars at Godin Tepe in Iran and at other sites in Transcaucasia and Turkey.' He also noted holes in Cretian Myrtos pithoi pots produced before firing and others from ancient Turkey and the Levant where the Phoenicians originated. All of which suggests the holed pots could have reached Alentejo 1000 years earlier than the Romans, via the Phoenicians.

Interestingly, McGovern's book cast some doubt on the possibility of these holes being used for tapping or draining wine, speculating that, 'it was difficult to imagine how wine could have been decanted or racked through them, as had been proposed for Godin Tepe vessels, without contaminating the wine with the lees.'

However, as previously discussed, typical *talha* practice is to pre-fill the bottom with stems, creating an excellent natural filter within the lower mass of 'lees' (*mae*/mother) that eliminates this issue. Whereas during initial draining, the first twenty or so liters runs a little cloudy, the remaining fifteen hundred drains completely clear. The original twenty are re-added into the top and come through clear as well.

In addition to this, Professor Virgílio Loureiro and Amareleja winemaker, José Piteira, have recreated another traditional Alentejo *talha* method of filtration, that bundled small, 5mm-wide reeds/dutch rush tubes together. These bundles are inserted into the hole after fermentation. Unexpectedly, this filtering greatly improves clarity over what was an already a more than acceptable practice.

As to whether clay winemaking pots may have existed in Alentejo before the Phoenicians showed up, Dr. Mkrtich Harutyunyan pointed me to several sources. Carolina López-Ruiz (2021) indicated Phoenicians traded with Alentejo's inland Tartessian tribes introducing improvements in pot firing and grape growing, along with various forms of transportable containers *amphorae*.

All of this suggests the Tartessians were already making wine in pots, growing grapes and had established the rudiments of wine culture in what would become future *talha* territory. What size, shape and kind of pots they were gets sketchier the earlier we go in time, so speculation is probably best left until a clearer picture emerges.

What it all definitely suggests is that the Romans arrived into an area that had been growing grapes and making wine in terracotta pots for hundreds, possibly thousands of years before.

The Yawning Gap

Which brings us back to the large historic gap in evidence for *talha* pots between Roman times and the 1600s, when production seems to have expanded, and when dating and place of manufacture started to appear in fully formed *talha* pots. Although 1200 years represents a lot of missing evidence, it may simply have been that there wasn't a lot of winemaking in *talha* pots outside of monasteries up until secular production took off in the 17th century. Natural attrition via explosions and cracking and *pés* application, may be the simplest explanation as to why so few pots may have survived during this period.

Professor Virgílio Loureiro is convinced that *talha* wine production was continuous at São Cucufate after Roman times, even during the Moorish occupation, where he believes there was a degree of toleration for Christian wine practices. Even probably during the really severe Caliphate period in the 1100s, they at least would have been used for vinegar production. The fact that nearby Vila de Frades was named for its wealth of friars suggests large *talha* may simply have been moved from São Cucufate as production expanded, into the village.

Countering the lack of larger Roman winemaking pots, Dr. Loureiro noted that many large Roman pots used for grain and olive oil storage have survived from antiquity, so they did at least exist back then. I also found sources indicating the Romans were transporting wine up the Guadiana River in 2000-liter pots.

Holy Grail

As this book was going to print, the holy grail seemed to pop up out of nowhere!

It turns out, the Faro Municipal Museum houses two larger, 1.5 meter high, Roman-era *dolia*. These radically change the story. Firstly, they are both more similarly sized and shaped to 1600-era Alentejo *talhas*, rather than the surviving *dolia* from São Cucufate and Ammaia.

More significantly, they had pre-fired holes, confirming there were holes in local pots during Portugal's Roman-era. Faro was not only Rome's most important Portuguese coastal city, but was an equally important trading center for both the Phoenicians and Tartessians. One mystery potentially solved.

Museu Municipal de Faro's single-holed Roman-era *dolium*, proving continual lineage between modern Portuguese *talha* and Roman-era pot forms. (A special thanks to the Museu Municipal de Faro for photo usage. All copyrights Museu Municipal de Faro).

Topping that, just hours before going to press, another breakthrough. Coming up trumps again, Dr. Mkrtich Harutyunyan directed me to a study (Dias Viegas, et al., 2007) that added a new twist. They gathered clay samples from 39 Roman-era *dolia* excavated in the coastal towns of Cadiz through Faro (including the two above) and at sites within the Guadalquivir River Valley, stretching deep within the heartland of the old Tartessian state. The gist of the study found that *dolia* were moving back and forth within this relatively large region, proved by a chemistry analysis of clay used in each pot which was traceable back to their original clay mines.

Suddenly I had a lightbulb moment.

Museu Municipal de Faro's rare three-holed Roman-era
dolium. This form may be linked to an even earlier Phoenician
period, given Faro's importance as a trading center then.
(Copyright Museu Municipal de Faro)

We have dates for many *talha* from the 1600s onward, but virtually no evidence for *talha* going back to 400 AD. What suddenly dawned on me was an equally large number of undated *talha* could easily be from that 400-1600 period - hiding in plain sight. The same chemical analysis could prove this is the case or at least where these 'unknowns' originated. It's entirely possible Roman-era *talha* are still being used throughout Alentejo without anyone realizing it.

At the very least, it's likely that later period *talha* do have a continuous link back to terracotta pots used during Alentejo Roman-era, and possibly to earlier periods as well.

Talha from 1600s at Outeiros Altos

The last of the last

Something I hadn't noticed in my early experiences with *talha* was that some had been made from concrete. Cuba's Monte Pedral *taberna* has the largest holding of these, where most are still making wine today. These appear to have been made around the time terracotta production ended in the 1920s.

The question is, did they accelerate the demise of clay *talha* or simply fill a gap after the great masters disappeared? XXVI Talha's booklet documents the 200 surviving *talha* in Vila Alva. Of these, 65% are clay made in the 17-20th centuries and 35% were made of reinforced concrete, all manufactured post-1930s in Vila Alva.

Contemporary commercial advertisements tout their robustness and resistance to exploding or cracking. Some offered higher volumes above 1500 liters as well. All must have been positive selling points and they may have continued to fill a niche for those still working *talha*. This was also the period when massive 10,000-20,000 liter concrete, squarish tanks were becoming common. Larger and more efficient, these tanks, in turn, would have trumped any advantages cement *talha* had to offer.

Future Talha Pot Production

In retrospect, it's odd that no one locally has re-established large-scale *talha* pot making in Alentejo. Given historic pots can sell for between 2000-3000 euros/dollars each there is clearly a ready market for them. Not to mention an even greater potential in the New World and elsewhere in Europe.

Concrete *talhas* at Monte Pedral *taberna*

The technology isn't that difficult to replicate, as testified by the *qvevri* pot makers still plying their trade in Georgia, all with long waiting lists. Given large numbers of historic *talha* pots to pattern off and a huge body of scientific information concerning modern ceramic manufacture to draw on, add in a growing market potential, it's a wonder each of Alentejo's traditional pot making centers isn't thriving again.

At least a couple of Portuguese have tried their hand at making big-assed old style pots recently; one locally in Vidigueira, Antonio Rocha, and another in the Tejo region to the north, José Figuereiro. Although they haven't mastered the art of making large *talha* yet, they will no doubt get there with a little more experience and a lot more trial and error.

I haven't visited Figuereiro yet, but have observed the quixotic endeavor of Antonio Rocha. He has taken up the challenge with virtually no background in pottery, firing or winemaking. His initial orders followed a commission from a local museum for display pots. To that end he learned the basics of shaping and firing pots, built a clever underground kiln and eventually filled those orders. Encountering problems with leakage, production of working pots have proved more elusive, needing further refinement of firing temperatures, clay sources and building techniques. The huge amount of time and effort he has put in so far suggests he will get there in the end.

Chapter Nine
Jupiter's Lift Off

Wow, it was stunning news when it surfaced back in 2021. Real rags-to-riches stuff. A wine produced in a *talha* from Portugal's Alentejo region, quickly sold out of its limited run of 650 bottles for 1000 euros apiece!

It was significant on many levels, beyond the eye-popping price.

Herdade do Rocim's Jupiter is certainly the most expensive wine produced in a clay vessel anywhere on earth, ever. Okay, MAYBE Caligula was drinking something more exclusive and relatively more expensive in his day and age. So let's dial that back to just: 'in modern times.'

Regardless, this not only proved that wines matured in terracotta can both evolve positively, along the lines of wines aged in wood, but also that this ancient Roman winemaking vessel can compete with the rarest and most expensive wines in the world.

It also proved that Alentejo's autochthonous grapes are as capable of high quality as any others from anywhere else; in this particular case, a unique, 80-120-year-old, field blended vineyard of varietals hardly anyone has heard of and fewer still can pronounce. This typical vineyard assemblage is also special for its long interconnection with local *talha* wine production, with some grapes possibly (probably?) linked back to pre-Roman-Iberian origins.

The union of the two also establishes a new concept of terroir. It's not simply about old endangered grapes that have not only survived, but thrived through adaptation to a specific place over a long time. Equally important is their follow-on interaction with an equally singular terroir-based vessel; where each pot is of a different size, shape, clay source and firing condition. Every *talha* is a terroir unto itself. One that can only be mastered through direct experience.

There are several other more trifling firsts. Jupiter was the most expensive release for any Portuguese still wine. And was from the under-known, underdog Alentejo region. There's also the hubbub surrounding Jupiter as news buzzed around social media for three months (more than 360,000+ purported hits), causing endless circular debates concerning whether it actually is/was worth the price or deserved the accolades...being from Portugal, Alentejo, *talha*, yaddayaddayadda. No doubt most of this by people who had never tasted it, nor understood the significance of its background.

For what it's worth, I love that this has happened.

There is a degree of serendipity to how Rocim's winemaker Pedro Ribeiro produced this wine. It began with the picking of Vinha de Micaela, a tiny (.36 hectare) 80+ year-old vineyard, scattered about with Moreto, Tinta Grossa, Trincadeira, Alicante Bouschet and others too few to count or bother identifying.

The parcel, adjacent to Rocim's home vineyard, was bought in 2015 and harvested shortly after for the first time. Lacking any track record, all of the grapes suddenly appeared at the winery, leaving Ribeiro scurrying for somewhere to co-ferment this small, oddball batch. Luckily the lot just happened to fit perfectly into three small early 19th century 600-liter *talhas*.

Ribeiro's original intentions were to bottle this as Vinho de Talha DOC.

As mentioned in previous chapters, the DOC regulations require wine to be held on skins at least until St. Martin's Day (Nov 11). Thereafter wines must be officially examined and certified before removal from skins to gain DOC status. Ribeiro intended to hold off inspection until bottling in March.

At the time of expected bottling, Ribeiro re-tasted the three *talha* and instantly realized one pot held the 'best wine I'd ever made.' Defying normal practice, Pedro decided to leave it and see how it evolved. Holding back a portion for topping up, he blended the rest into his normal Vinho de Talha DOC wine.

Ageing wine in *talha*, indeed amphora generally, is largely uncharted territory. *Talhas* are primarily fermentation vessels, with wine traditionally drunk up within a year - more often sooner.

The caveat here is that terracotta pots allow around twice as much (or more) oxygen through their walls as an oak barrel. Hence, they need to be monitored closely for oxidation to avoid any sudden tipping point ruining the wine. Another issue is the wide, irregular mouth which is not easily sealed air tight for regular topping up. A third problem is that no two *talhas* are alike: different sized and shaped, different internal convection currents, different clay sourcing, wall thickness and firing conditions. Each *talha* dictates its own winemaking parameters.

All that said, where in modern times the design isn't normally used for longer term maturation, ALL of the great 19th century Alentejan '1st growths' (Jose de Sousa, Tapada do Chaves, Quinta do Carmo (now Dona Maria), Mouchao) made wine in *talha* with a reputation for ageing well. Of these, only Jose de Sousa continued carrying the torch into the late 20th century, albeit in the 1980s they shifted to small oak barrique maturation.

I've tasted many Jose de Sousa's *talha* wines back into the 1940s, and most are still very drinkable. Most recently, in August 2021 I drank a superb 1940 in an Evora restaurant. And I've tasted Georgian *qvevri* wine that had been aged in clay for seven years that remained remarkably fresh. So clay can age.

However, while maturation in *talha* clearly IS possible, the 'modern' DOC rules are designed for early drinking wines. A lack of both ancient and modern practical advice on how to mature wine in *talha*, has created a new frontier.

Ribeiro has been at the forefront of pushing these boundaries over the last eight years. Beyond the 20,000 bottles of Rocim's red and white Amphora (Vinho de Talha DOC) and another 8000 *talha*-made, 'Fresh from Amphora' wines, and Bojador Reserva Vinho de Talha DOC, Rocim also produces 5500 bottles of 'Clay Aged' wine. The latter is kept in barrique sized pots, not dissimilar to clay barrels produced in Alentejo during the 19th century.

So Rocim's Jupiter was no fluke.

Checking the future Jupiter religiously in 2016, Ribeiro was surprised (sometimes shocked) by the lack of oxidation and continued positive evolution. One year carried into another and eventually, after 48 months in clay and a further year in bottle, the wine was released.

Here's the rub. Because the wine was racked off skins without being observed and certified for Vinho de Talha DOC, Jupiter couldn't legally use the word *talha*, hence it had to be labeled 'amphora' made. It was a bit of an own goal for Vinho de Talha DOC regulations. The most expensive, most famous *talha*-made wine ever, knocked down to lowly 'amphora' wine status.

So far the wine is a one off. In the chaos of the 2015 harvest nothing was recorded as to what part of the vineyard went into which *talha*. Since then Ribeiro has systematically tried to rediscover the 2015 mix without luck. Humbled, but undeterred, he has been methodically narrowing in on probables and, nevertheless, says he 'will make it again.'

Eventually 650 bottles (of 800 total) of Jupiter were released June 2021 as the first in Cláudio Martin's 'Wines From Another World' collection. 500 bottles sold out in 3 days and the remainder within 2 months.

As for the wine? My initial impression, albeit from a brief tasting over lunch with Ribeiro, was that it was pitch perfect. It was a remarkably well balanced wine compared to any wine, not just to other *talha* wine. Perhaps more so specifically because *talha* can be so cranky and unpredictable to produce.

– Later, I was able to spend a quiet evening with a whole bottle and found Jupiter, half-way down. It was ultra-faithful to Videgueira's traditional, field blended red grapes. Offering up a rich mix of red and black fruit aromas, similar flavors bled into one another, enriched by a minerally, graphite gloss, everything playing out in a harmonious mix of its four primary grape components. Trincadeira contributed florals and depth, Alicante Bouschet adding color and acidity, Tinta Grossa laying down tannic structure and tart cherry notes, and Moreto offered still more cherry characters, finesse and finish.

Jupiter was a really fulfilling mouthful from beginning to end. Even thrilling at times. I especially liked the lack of oak polluting the pure fruit and skin tannins. Its *talha* had delivered just enough oxygen to dress the structure and polish the surface with a slick and smooth gloss. Equally impressive were differing grape tannins stacked in, front to back, and laid on through a multi-layered attack.

Texturally it entered with a plush mouthfeel and left with a long tapered finish, shot through with firm, fine tannins and requisite acidity. Concentrated from the start, it built, indeed exploded mid-mouth and welled up, ending with a delicate juiciness and more than ample residual flavors.

Is a bottle worth a grand? Is any wine really worth a grand? Jupiter is certainly as rare and singular as most other grand wines out there. If I had a spare grand to spend, I'd probably have bought one. But that was and is a fairly insurmountable 'if'.

From my own experience having tasted dozens of terracotta wines going back 80 years, Jupiter really was pitch perfect. Structurally there is no reason it shouldn't evolve into something remarkable in old age. Maybe one of my yet-to-be conceived grandchildren can weigh in someday on how well it compared to that Jose De Sousa 1940 I drank, one night in Evora.

Chapter 10
A New Concept of Terroir & Grand Cru

Terroir is one way to explain how grapes express themselves through a final wine. The traditional concept of terroir revolves around a vineyard's soil and grapes, its position on earth, its seasonal weather and the human input it receives over that time. *Talha's* old mixed vineyards - fine tuned over centuries - create perfect expressions of their space and time, consistently, year in, year out. Arguably, that specific expression is on par with the predictable designation of 'Grand Cru' vineyards in other parts of the world like Burgundy or Barolo.

Amplifying this aspect of unique, biological originality, *talha* up the ante with their own unique terroir; one bound by size and shape, age, original firing conditions, the original source of clay and the earthen-mineral content creating that clay.

Talha pots are bespoke environments that over time have not only taken on their own distinctive characteristics but also produce distinctive characteristics in wine. Each pot requires a few years of winemaking experience to understand how much oxygen the pot allows in during fermentation, the influence of its internal convection currents, and how all that impacts on both fermentation and maturation. Just as important to the equation is how a *talha* deals with differing kinds of grapes, their seasonal growth pattern and harvesting conditions. Taken together, all this multiplies terroir by a factor or 2.

It turns out this total concept has quite naturally already made its way into *talha* production. Winemakers are matching specific parcels of vines to specific *talha* based on their experience of how they churn out wine together.

Talha are proving to be especially adept at containing small parcels of special vineyards. Given that most old vines are in tiny plots under an acre, the plots can often be perfectly matched to typical *talha* pot size from 600-1500 liters. Rocim's Jupiter, Jose de Sousa's Puro and the old vine wines of Rui Reguenga, Esporão and Susana Esteban have all successfully testified to this potential.

This new concept of total terroir is not only here to stay, but bound to grow in future.

Chapter 11
Final Thoughts on Beautiful Pots

There is an undeniable beauty captured in *talha* pots, as pleasing to the eye as they are functional. Formed by hands, coordinated by eyes and intellect, they take us back before the age of machines and manufactured uniformity, offering an element of humanity that isn't often found in the modern world of sterile wine technology.

It's always intriguing to watch peoples' first impressions of *talha*. They love to touch them, walk around them, just be amongst them... *Talha* are as calming as they are awe-inspiring.

Working *talha* at Cooperativa Vidigueira

Like massive stone sculptures or megalithic structures, *talha* inhabit space monumentally. A winery filled with *talha* doesn't feel like a factory, it feels more like a church or a cathedral - one dedicated to craftsmanship where art and patience still rule.

Talha at Fitapreta

Each *talha* casts an aura of silent mystery. Each with its own story to tell. Stories that go beyond speech, spanning years of service to generations across centuries. A silent service followed by subsequent periods of abandonment and, ultimately, burial under the paths of progress.

But now they are back, newly appreciated for how wonderfully concise they once were at making wine from a specific place and time. The world's most perfect machine for making wine is back in action.

Clay is here to stay.

Much-loved and much-signed *talha* at Pais das Uvas

PART 2: THE PRODUCERS

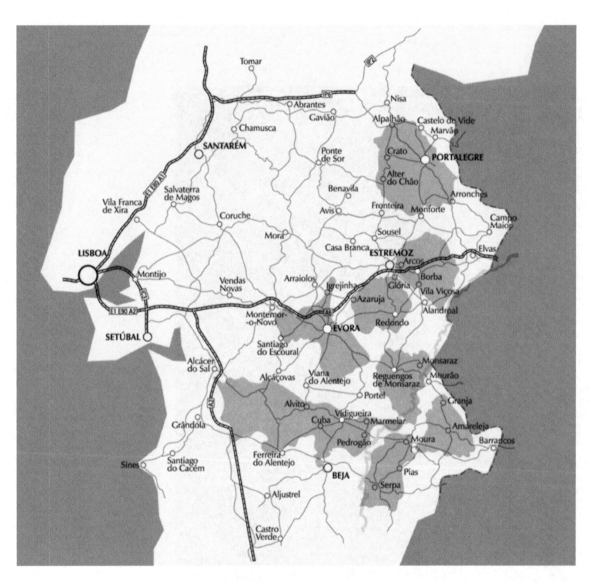

Map of Alentejo DOC regions from from top to bottom:
Portalegre, Borba, Redondo, Evora, Reguengos, Vidigueira, Granja-Amareleja, and Moura.
Map provided by CVRA

Chapter 12
ACV

Sub-region: Vidigueira
Owner/Winemaker: Alexandre Frade
Address: Praça 25 de abril 12, 7960-421 Vila de Frades, Portugal
Phone: +351 935 109 541
Email: geral@vinhodetalha.pt
Website: https://vinhodetalha.com/Store/en/
General Information:
50 *talha*, 750 to 1800 liters, oldest dated 1856
Talha are epoxy lined, not *pés*
Founding member of Association of Vinho de Talha Producers (APVT)

After spending most of his life working as a professional accountant, in his later years Alexandre Frade returned to the *talha* wine culture he knew during his childhood. His ACV adega faces the Vila de Frades main square, with *talha* lining the walls inside, its hand-painted signs and modest décor harking back to a time when *talha* were central to Vila de Frades life. Now, as then, he serves his young wine to customers direct from the *talha*, but also sells older wine by the bottle.

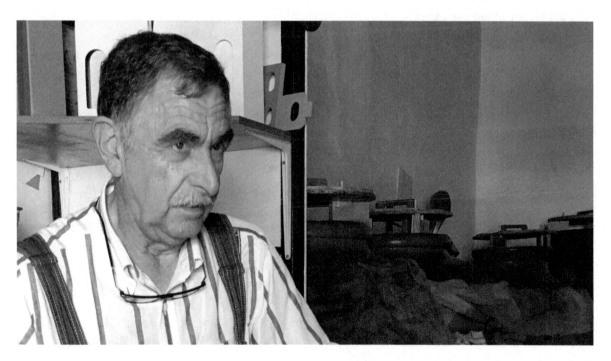

Alexander Frade in his adega

Frade is a larger than life character, loud, not shy, highly opinionated and just as highly animated. When I first met him he was on his belly in the middle of his adega, with his arm down a hole up to its pit, trying to unclog a drain. Achieving sudden success, he popped back to his feet, all the while declaiming and explaining and speculating on subjects ranging from how the words Portuguese *talha* and Spanish *tinajas* derived from Roman for 'big pots', to his irritation at people saying *talha* wine can't age and his passionate aim to prove that wrong. Then back to how the Roman soldiers watered down their wine to make an easier drinking rose. And then opining on Trincadeira, a grape he considered to be very female, elegant, but so much trouble!

Thing is, I suspect anyone walking in the door of his tiny adega to taste a few wines before buying one, would probably receive a similar range of rapid fire topics tossed out to accompany their sniffing and slurping.

Frade's credentials are long-lived having first worked as a 12-year-old in his father's *talha taberna* in Beja during the late 1960s. He recalls his father transferring wine from large *talha* every night to replenish the small *talha* that served his customers the following day. This, like much of the history he relates, comes first hand.

During the mid-1970s he watched as bottling arrived and forever changed the nature of *talha tabernas*. The elimination of oxidation, bringing longer lasting freshness, consistency and greater uniformity irrevocably changed wine styles. Taverns increasingly abandoned *talha* winemaking and they themselves dwindled in size and number until almost all had disappeared.

Although Frade wasn't part of the wine making nucleus of the original Vitifrades group that promoted DOC certification, several are close old friends dating from when they all ran together in their 20s. He supported their cause from its earliest days and promised that someday he would return to *talha* winemaking. And so he did, producing his first 'official' Vinho de Talha DOC wine in 2015.

Very much a staunch traditionalist, currently ACV has a 50 *talha* capacity, ranging in size from 750 to 1800 liters, with the oldest branded from 1856. How many are filled each year depends on the nature of the season, ranging from 3000 bottles at worst and 12,000 in the best years. In cool, wet 2021, for example, he only used 24 *talha*. The number used and the size and shape of each are precisely matched to Frade's intimate knowledge of his grapes and how they've grown each year.

All wines are kept on 'mother' until St. Martin's Day, then transferred to a clean *talha* for further ageing before bottling in May, purposefully leaving in some sediment. Wines are generally released after two years.

One of Frade's bugbears is overcoming the belief that *talha* wine doesn't age well. He has been keen to prove otherwise, noting he currently has 5 to 6-year old wines in his cellar that are still evolving. Indeed, after making *talha* wines for six years following traditional techniques, quite late in life, he returned to university to formally study winemaking. His intent was to understand the scientific reasons behind how to extend the maturity of *talha* wine without the use of chemicals.

His current theory is that *talha* render a more complex phenolic (tannic) composition, partly due to the shape creating a natural battonage on lees which, by its nature, is a highly anti-oxidative process. He also reckons the seven week fermentation with caps (skins) punched down four times a day helps create a raft of complex, antioxidant-rich tannins.

ACV draws fruit from an old five-hectare vineyard of mixed whites grown near Vidigueira (Antão Vaz, Roupeiro, Mantuedo, Diagalves, Larião, Perrum and others). He noted in the past the old mixed vineyard was primarily older local grape varieties, but over time this shifted toward a dominance of Antao Vaz. His reds also come from a mixed vineyard, near - considerably hotter - Moura (Tricadeira, Tinta Roriz, Moreto, Tinto Grossa). Some of his vines are over 100 years old.

And finally, what goes around, comes around… the Frade family have come full circle once again. Having skipped a generation, Alexandre's son runs a Michelin-rated *taberna* in Lisbon, O Frade in Belem, focused on selling *talha* wine to accompany traditional, family-style dishes.

Wines

ACV Peculiar 2017 16%!!! Vinho de Talha DOC. This blend of Aragonez and Trincadeira, from a hot year and hot climate Moura vineyard, is a whopping big wine: spirit-ridden nose, a full body laden with alcoholic glycerine and

Frade's *talha* are dressed in water soaked cloth *farrapo* to lower internal fermentation temperatures 4-5C

a dry, hot fire-breathing finish. Unexpectedly it offered relatively fine tannins. Frades suggests this wine could age for 20 years and needs at least two hours to open up properly. I didn't have time to wait and see. However, I did find after 30 minutes the wine did gather a bit more minerality and cooked-fruit characters emerged. The wine wasn't oxidized, but sun-baked fruit gave it that impression. As air opened up the fruit it seemed less fiery. A hard one to rate. Not my style, as I crave more acidity, but I can see it might do well on a cold winter night alongside a mature chunk of strong cheese.

ACV 1856 Branco 2018 13% Vinho de Talha DOC. This blend of Antão Vaz and Arinto was grown near Vidigueira and wears a bright amber color. Full bodied and rounded, with a tight streak of firm acidity and intriguing green tea-like flavors. Bottled with minimal sulphites. It's very grippy and very much a gastronomic style. 88/100

ACV Antigas 2018 13%. This is quite an extraordinary wine that doused expectations. It wears an amber color shifted with a reddish peach-like blush, that suggested 'orange' wine-like apple skin aromas and flavors and hard, malic acid, tannic bite. But it wasn't like that at all. True there were hints of apple skin aromas, but they were subtle, buried within a mineral gloss. Again expecting a harder edged mouthfeel, this didn't appear supplanted by a rounded, plush mouthfeel, laced with pear-apricot flavors, integrated acidity and fine skin tannins. ACV's pitch is in making *talha* wines that can age. Tasted four years after birth, this proved the point. 89

Chapter 13
Cooperativa Adega de Borba

Sub-region: Borba
Winemaker: Oscar Gato
Address: Largo Gago Coutinho e Sacadura, Cabral 25, Apartado 20, 7151-913 Borba, Portugal
Email: geral@adegaborba.pt
Phone: (00351) 268 891 660
General Information: owners: 270 growers, no use of *pés*
Talha: 14, also 1200L oak barrels
Vineyards: 2,220 hectares

Talha at Adega de Borba

Like Vidigueira's Coop, Cooperativa Adega de Borba is both an historically important center for *talha* winemaking and a major producer of wine for all of Portugal. Indeed, Portuguese consumers have long recognized Adega de Borba for their consistently good quality, reasonably priced wines (10 million bottles!), especially their reds.

The *talha* built into the Adega's early-14th-century fortified walls indicate they've been around for at least seven centuries. But there is little reason to doubt that *talha* kept the Roman stonemasons, who carved high quality marble out of nearby quarries, happy from much earlier times.

Oscar Gato of Adega Borba

Borba itself is a key city in the 'northern' *talha* culture that stretches west into Arcos and Estremoz and further north into the mountains around Portalegre. These northerners inhabited higher elevations and experienced cooler climates, which favored different mixes of grapes from their southern neighbors. All these regions sourced their *talha* from master potters based near Borba, in Campo Maior and Amieira do Tejo.

Cooperativa Adega de Borba's winemaker Oscar Gato reckons the beginning of the decline of *talha* began in the late 19th century with the introduction of concrete tanks. *Talha* co-existed with concrete until the advent of the coop in 1955. Thereafter *talha* went into serious decline, with grapes instead destined to be made into wine at the cooperative.

Gato explained that the cooperative was originally established in 1955 by 45 producers who were tired of being exploited by negotiants buying up their wine, blending it into their brands and collecting all the profit. Banding together to gain scale, they cut out the middlemen, and invested in new technology, bottling collectively and dividing the profits between themselves.

In 2014, Gato re-established *talha* wine production at the cooperative. Ironically, this was around the time I visited the last of nearby Arcos's wonderfully authentic, tiny neighborhood tascas, owned by Antonio Gato (see opening *tasca* chapter; Antonio it turns out, is Oscar's uncle). Smaller scale *talha* production had continued in *tabernas* but this diminished over the years, with Gato's uncle's small scale *tasca* being one of the last holdouts.

Antonio has since retired and, sadly, his *tasca* has now closed its doors. But across the street in Senhor Gato's adega, an old 1670 *talha* is hidden away. We can only hope that Gato's *tasca* will find someone eager to bring it back to life and this beautiful *talha* will find its way back into use.

Borba's grapes are grown on a high plateau between 400-500m. Like all of the northern *talha* enclaves, this higher elevation creates a wetter, cooler climate, often with a 20C-degree difference between day and night temperature. Gato selects grapes for balance and natural acidity. All that and a longer growing season favor freshly fruited, elegantly styled reds, which, in Borba's case, make up 70% of production.

Since 2014 production has ranged between 3000-5000 bottles of red per year. 2021 marks the first production of around 1000 bottles of white *talha* wine. All of the coop's *talha* wine is certified Vinho de Talha DOC. The only non-traditional practice is the introduction of stainless steel cooling rods into *talha* to lower temperatures, which makes for fresher, fruitier styles. They also don't use *pés*, which adds to the emphasis on pure fruit characters.

Although Borba own 14 large (1000-1800L) old *talha* dating from between 1860-1890, they only use five currently. As the market for *talha* wine grows, the cooperative has a huge potential, given its massive source of old vineyards and pots, to restore what was once the prevailing wine style of Borba and its surrounding region.

Talha wines

Talhas de Borba Branco 2021 Vinho de Talha DOC. Usually a blend of around 60% Rabo de Ovelha, 30% Roupeira, 10% Tamarez. Quite an exotic and aromatic wine style with intriguing vanilla and banana high tones. Obviously from the fruit, not oak barrels! Full bodied, softly textured, welcoming with a light, crisp-apple fresh underlying acidity. A very happy sort of wine that can put a big grin on your face. Drinking perfectly in early March just nine months after its birth. This is a shooting star of a wine, best consumed as early in its first year as possible. 88/100

Talhas de Borba Tinto 2020 13.5% Vinho de Talha DOC. A big generously fruited, co-fermented blend of Trincadeira 40%, Castelão 40% and Alicante Bouschet 20%. It checks all the right boxes: co fermented, low intervention, natural filtering... Clean, fresh, spicy aromas follow on in the mouth creamy smooth, seamless texture laced with juicy fruits and fine acidity. A really nice wine: focused, precise, pure and persistent. I've tasted this wine 3 times and it just gets better and better. 89

Talhas de Borba Tinto 2019 13.5% Vinho de Talha DOC. A co-fermented blend of Trincadeira, Castelão and Alicante Bouschet. From a hotter year, picked earlier with a shorter growing season. Warmer season created, roasted fruit characters. Fuller, bodied richer than 2020 and 2018, with firmer acidity and dusty, dryer tannins. 87

Talhas de Borba Tinto 2018 13.5% Vinho de Talha DOC. From a cooler, longer season, the latest picked in the last 10 years. A blend of Trincadeira with more Castelão and less Alicante Bouschet this vintage. A fresher style with higher acidity. More floral, fruitier in mouth with firm acidity and very firm tannins. Fine bodied with a nice degree of elegance. 88

Chapter 14
Cortes de Cima

Sub-region: Reguengos
Address: 7960-189 Vidigueira, Portugal
Owners/Winemaker: Jørgensen family, Anna Jørgensen
Phone: (+351) 914672845
Email: visits@cortesdecima.pt
Website: https://cortesdecima.com/#

Hans and Carrie Jørgensen sailed around the world searching for a place to grow their favorite grape, Syrah. Landing in the Algarve and finding their way into the expansive landscape of Alentejo, in 1988 they established a vineyard on bare land and rebuilt an abandoned ruin to live in. Hans, a Dane who made his fortune as an engineer in Malaysia, and Carrie, bringing her native Californian free spiritedness, the two were maverick outsiders from the start. These New Worlders brought something different to Alentejo, while Alentejo, the tolerant 'wild west' of Portugal, allowed them space to do their own thing.

Mid-summer tasting with Hans and Carrie Jorgensen at Cortes de Cima

From the start Cima's wines were technologically driven and unabashedly New World in style - focused more on French grapes rather than Portuguese grapes and local traditions. In the early days the DOC didn't allow Syrah as an official grape, so Cima labeled theirs 'Incognito.' Later the DOC changed its mind and made it a sanctioned grape. So far Cortes de Cima have chosen to remain outside Alentejo's DOC system, although that may change in future.

Over time there has been an evolution in Cortes de Cima's relationship with Alentejo. As locals came to appreciate Cima's irreverent marketing, innovation and experimentation, Cortes de Cima in turn have absorbed or adapted some of Alentejo's distinctive grapes and traditional styles into their mix.

One big change has been a shift in their use of *talha* - from architectural decoration back into a revolutionary winemaking vessel. This change is driven by their daughter, Anna Jørgensen, who returned home after completing a viticulture and oenology degree from University of Adelaide, not to mention having worked in Australia's four main regions (Barossa, McLaren Vale, Adelaide Hills, Hunter Valley), New Zealand, California's Russian River and France (Burgundy and Northern Rhone).

Anna Jorgensen checking grapes in Cortes de Cima *talha*

Where the previous winemaker had experimented with maturing wine in small clay 100-160 liter jugs, Jørgensen moved away from these, not liking the results. Her team compared wines aged in oak versus the jars, finding the latter developed too quickly: 'after about 10 months they appeared drier and duller compared to the oak aged equivalent.' They proved difficult to clean, too porous from low firing temperatures and fragile; in particular, the lip where the bung sits was far too easily broken. On top of that, they were too expensive and labor intensive compared to *talha*. *Talha*, at ten times the size, were also far less oxidative.

Jørgensen came to see *talha* as 'a creative space for us to explore,' sometimes following the DOC guidelines, sometimes not. When I last visited in August 2021, their current Daqui 2021 sat bubbling away in a big *talha*, alongside smaller *talhas* containing a white Viognier and a Palhete (traditional blend of red and white wine) made with whole clustered Syrah, co-fermented with Viognier. They also had a *talha* driven Petillant Naturel produced from Touriga Franca.

They consider their mainline Daqui (meaning 'from here') to be a 'moving' interpretation of *talha*. While their old 2000-liter *talha* remains the constant, the grapes may change. One year a 50/50 blend of Aragonez and Trincadeira, another year, Touriga Franca.

The 2020 Daqui probably could have qualified for DOC status, given it followed all the rules. Organically farmed Touriga Franca, it used 1/3 whole bunches to line the bottom for later natural filtration. It was foot-trodden to create gentle extraction during fermentation, didn't use temperature control or chemical additions and went through a traditional three-month maceration. On St. Martin's day (11th November) it was drained through the *mãe* or mother into a tank, given a touch of sulfur and left to stabilize naturally during winter. Eventually 1200 bottles were hand-bottled in the spring.

Although Cortes de Cima came to the *talha* party relatively late, their outsider's perspective is producing an interesting mixed approach to modern and old practices. One stream follows the classical traditional formula of making wine using local grapes in *talha* within the St. Martin's Day time frame, while a second, parallel stream is exploring how French grapes can be reshaped by *talha's* ancient technology.

Anyone who has seen the row of empty *talha* out behind the winery knows there are more interesting things to come.

The wines

Cortes de Cima Daqui Branco 2022. 100% Viognier, similarly produced as the 2021 below, except pulled off the mother early in mid-October to reduce skin-derived bitterness. A mix of spicy apple pie aromas with cinnamon high tones, pear flavors, and bouncy acidity 88/100

Cortes de Cima Daqui Branco 2021. This is an outside-the-box, *talha*-made wine using 100% Viognier, 30% whole bunch fermented. It is the first year they've applied a beeswax and resin mixture of *pés*. A year in, it is has come together nicely with spicy honeyed aromas, tart lemony flavors and firm, but fine. 88

Cortes de Cima Daqui 2020. Adelaide meets Alentejo. A big bouncy fruity mouthful, brimming with black fruit and mulberry characters kept in check with an edgy, tart streak of juicy acidity. A new lively spirited form of Tareco. 88

Cortes de Cima Palhete 2022. This is a wild new take on traditional Palhete and its mix of co-fermented white and red grapes, this time taking a cue from the Rhone Valley's Côte-Rotie mix of whole bunch Syrah and Viognier. I sampled this in its baby stage and it was still showing quite reductive toasted aromas, although promising lots of juicy red cherry, red fruit aromas and flavors in future, once it loses its puppy fat. 89

Chapter 15
Herdade do Esporão

Sub-region: Reguengos
Winemaker: Joao Ramos (previously Sandra Alves and David Baverstock)
Address: Apartado 31, 7200-999, Reguengos de Monsaraz
Distrito de Évora, Alentejo, Portugal
Phone: (+351) 266 509 280
Email: reservas@esporao.com
Website: https://www.esporao.com/en/

Herdade do Esporão is an old, old place, but with a more recent history ever full of new ideas. Known for their fresher, fruitier, consumer-friendly wine styles delivered through contemporary branding and labeling, Esporão helped establish Alentejo as an important producer of consistently clean, ripe wine at bargain prices both within Portugal and abroad. Many credit Esporão with leading the vanguard of producers that brought 'modern' large scale, technologically driven wine production and international wine styles to Alentejo in the late 1980s and early 1990s.

Driving much of this innovation was (now retired) Australian winemaker David Baverstock, who actively championed many of the standardized aspects of 'New World' styling: French grapes, new oak barrels, stainless steel tanks, temperature controlled fermentation, inoculated yeast, etc…all married back into Alentejo's local grapes and growing conditions. In a sense, recreating Alentejo as Europe's answer to Australia's Barossa Valley.

One of the most important aspects of Baverstock's innovative work was his systematic development of 100% varietal wines from Portuguese grapes. Previously these had been anonymous components of traditional blends, the parts generally being considered less important than the whole. The positive aspect of deconstructing these blends back into their individual components was a new understanding of each grape's strong and weak points. This in turn, allows each to either stand on its own as a single varietal or be reassembled in new ways on the basis of newly discovered knowledge. In some ways, it took an outsider like Baverstock to help rediscover what made Alentejo tick.

Over the last decade or so Esporão, David Baverstock, Sandra Alves (who followed his retirement), and current winemaker, Joao Ramos, have undergone a sea change of sorts, following a steady evolution away from 'internationalist' styling, back toward Alentejo's traditional wine production and the smaller, more intimate, locally oriented culture that surrounds it.

Their commitment to *talha* is just one example. Esporão have refocused their direction towards promoting a more holistic approach to sustainability on a broad front. Not just committing to Alentejo's environment, but also its traditions, history, culture and the economic viability of its people. Their published manifesto takes a page right out of Slow Food's Slow Wine movement: 'To be a family company that is economically, socially and environmentally sustainable, capable of providing unique products and experiences that improve people's lives.'

This philosophy is universally applied to what has become a very large operation covering 700 hectares of vineyards, olive groves and cork trees. All are farmed under organic methods and integrated production, working forty grape varieties and four types of olives. Much care has been taken to encourage ever more biodiversity through the establishment of a small lake and marsh. All of this is actively promoted through their wine tourism program based within the winery, restaurant and tasting room complex.

One unusual aspect is a tip towards ancient history. In the midst of planting vineyards in 1996 at nearby newly acquired Herdade dos Perdigões, they discovered a 4000-6000-year-old Neolithic village, megaliths and ceremonial necropolis, covering 16 hectares. Esporão offered ongoing financial support for archeological excavations, and it has since been declared a National Monument, with artifacts housed in Herdade do Esporão's original 13th century defensive tower, Perdigões Archeological Complex Museum.

All of which leads back to Esporão's *talha* wine production.

Concrete tanks, *lagars*, and *talha*

In a sense, it is a logical and natural progression from both Esporão and Baverstock's technological development from stainless steel and oak barrels, through to fermentation in massive concrete tulip-shaped tanks which show Portuguese grapes in a more neutral light, and onward into the more recent revival of clay pot technologies that are both historically and materially more specific to Alentejo. Old *talha* simply became the next frontier to conquer.

All Herdade do Esporão's *talha* wines follow the Vinho de Talha DOC guidelines and are certified. What is most interesting about their production is their choice of grapes and vineyards.

Both their white and red wines are non-traditional in being single varieties, Roupeiro and Moreto, and from the (sometimes super) hot Granja-Amareleja sub-region. Much more unusual - indeed extremely rare - is that grapes are from 'ungrafted' vines grown on sandy soil (many speculate that ungrafted vines produce purer characters). Esporão's third *talha* wine is a traditional field blend of 'old vine' red grapes from the cooler Portalegre region to the north.

All three wines are as distinct from one another as they are from other producers' Vinho de Talha DOC wine, but at the same time they are clearly within the bounds of that tradition. Where Esporão puts its mark on the wines is the seriousness of their intent in producing the complexity and refinement expected from their highest quality conventionally made wines.

White Wines

Esporão Roupeiro 2019 13.5% Vinho de Talha DOC. Grown on 50-year-old ungrafted vines in sandy soil in hot Granja-Amareleja region and naturally fermented. Delicately floral reminiscent of green flower stems, followed with clean, slick, smooth textures. Rounded and nicely weighted in the mouth with fine balancing acidity, good length and steely minerality throughout. With airing, wine extends flavor length that develops an interesting fruit sweetness and ever longer flavor length. 95/100

Esporão Roupeiro 2018 13.5% Vinho de Talha DOC. Grown on ungrafted vines in sandy soil in hot Granja-Amareleja region and naturally fermented. Deep golden color coming on with age. Initially it has a slightly sweet baseline aromas of green vegetables with dried green herb high notes. With airing, this gains a high-toned spiciness as well. Full bodied, densely textured and concentrated, all carried over through a long, fine, slickly viscous, gently tapered, melt-away finish. A complex, interesting wine made for food, but worth contemplating in a large well-focused glass. With decanting, it shifts yet again toward apple skin/cooked apple characters. 24 hours later it becomes a well integrated, compact wine with fine skin tannins and well-balanced acidity. 96

Red Wines

Esporão Moreto 2020 Vinho de Talha DOC unreleased sample. An interesting mix of honeyed red cherry cough drops. Quite broad in the mouth, this knits together with tight, bitter cherry acidity. After airing, full-bodied, packed with dried and fresh blackberry, black and cherry flavors. Dusty tannins. Flavors hang on the tongue a long time. 24 hours later it still has that honeyed cherry aroma, but everything is more integrated and smoother. Quite slick finish, with just enough acidity. Dried fruit/cherry characters throughout. 3rd night open! Quite liked it at that point. Acidity has emerged, along with dusty tannins to firm up structure. Dried cherry and honey characters remain, but better integrated now. Good wine. It just needs time and oxygen to show its best. 91

Esporão Moreto 2019 14% Vinho de Talha DOC. Granja-Amareleja. Made from 80 year old ungrafted vines on sandy soil and naturally fermented. Opens with spicy red fruit aromas, then leads right into a mix of fresh and dried cherry flavors bound into firm, dusty tannins. A terrific little wine with great concentration, fruit transparency, pleasing spiky rustic tannins and sharp acidity bolstering juicy fruits. Doesn't taste like it's from a hot year in a hot climate! 89

Esporão Vinho de Talha Vinhas Velhas 2015 14% Vinho de Talha DOC. Produced from 60-year-old field blend of Trincadeira, Aragonez, Castelão vines from the cooler Portalegre region. Made in a *pés* lined *talha* dated 1843, fermented with indigenous yeast ferment and taken off its 'mother' November 26. A complex mix of baseline black and red fruit aromas cast with an interesting mineral graphite gloss. A beautifully textured wine, seamlessly laced with a mix of red and black fruit flavors, with perfectly balanced acidity and tannin support. Marked by expansive, indeed, explosive mid-palate, with long lasting flavors. Pitch perfect balance, drinking beautifully now and for more years to come. Impressive wine. 98

Chapter 16
Fitapreta

Sub-region: Evora
Address: Paço do Morgado de Oliveira, EM527 KM10, Nossa Senhora da Graça do Divor 7000-016 Évora
Owner/winemaker: Antonio Mançanita
Phone: (+351) 915 880 095
Email: Adega@Fitapreta.com
Website: https://www.antoniomacanita.com/en/wines/fitapreta

Fitapreta's agro-engineer winemaker Antonio Mançanita is a free thinker who is willing to consider new solutions to old problems and just as happy challenging conventional thinking, sometimes from outside the box, sometimes from within. Initially educated and trained in Portugal, he broadened his perspective working in California, Bordeaux and Australia. Along the way he developed a close friendship with a like-minded English viticulturist named David Booth, and the two founded the Fitapreta project in 2004, making their first wine in Alentejo that year.

Antonio Mançanita in his tasting room

Fitapreta's formative period paralleled the Californian *garagistas* movement, buying in grapes from interesting vineyards and then making wine in borrowed facilities. The project grew by leaps and bounds during the 2000s, creating a number of novel and innovative wines from rare, unusual or endangered local varieties from old vineyards. These were bottled under innovative names and marketing, and eventually grew into four wine brands produced in the Azores, Douro and Alentejo.

Fitapreta old castle and modern winery near Evora

Then in 2008, while working with biodynamic-inspired concrete eggs in California, Mançanita had a light bulb moment. He'd seen something like this before back in Portugal, although in a considerably more ancient, upside-down form, and made from clay.

Returning to Alentejo in 2010, he took a pioneering stab at working with *talha*. Significantly, Fitapreta's first Branco de Talha was produced before Vinho de Talha DOC regulations were formally established.

Following David Booth's tragic premature death in 2012, Fitapreta eventually found a permanent home at Paço do Morgado de Oliveira in 2016. This magnificent 14th century palace just north of Evora is surrounded by extensive vineyards on gentle slopes. Counterpointing the palace, across its courtyard they've built a tastefully designed 'minimalist' cork and reconstituted-wood-clad, gravity-fed winery with a glass-walled tasting room that offers amazing views of nearby ruins. The project remains a work in progress, with the addition of another 20 hectare property with 50-year-old vines and the palace's disused original cellars in the process of being converted back over to *talha* wine production. *Talha* restored, once again, to their rightful place.

Fitapreta make a wide range of wine styles using a variety of methods and technologies, both modern and old, ranging between stainless steel tanks, oak barrels, extended skin contact, *talha* and, even, Jerez's flor yeast fermentation method used for making fino sherry. Mançanita would be the first to admit he does not follow a pure, traditionalist approach to *talha* production. Some whites are crushed and pressed and separated from skins before going into *talha* for fermentation, others are fermented with a month or two of skin contact, then moved to stainless steel for a year of ageing, and still others might maintain skin contact until April. Everything depends on the fruit and the season and what technique Mançanita thinks will serve the wine best. This approach treats *talha* more as a technology harnessed to produce desired results in an end wine, rather than a wine style dependent on strict adherence to a cultural tradition the DOC formula is designed to preserve.

The irony here is that because their first Branco de Talha wine predates the establishment of formal regulations for Vinhos de Talha DOC, Fitapreta's non-certified *talha*-made wines are legally allowed to use the term '*talha*' freely on their label. This allows Fitapreta a unique degree of creative freedom no other Alentejo winery is afforded, whereas all other non-certified, *talha*-made wines must be designated as 'amphora' made.

Most of Fitapreta's *talha* wine is white, except for a single red, with all of the grapes grown organically. Natural ferments are the norm, employing yeast that is started in each vineyard 4 or 5 days before harvest, a liter of which is placed in each *talha* to help supercharge the fermentation's start. *Pés* is not used because Mançanita wants pure terracotta contact, gaining the polished texture from oxygen transfer, while avoiding the *pés* flavoring.

Other, more unconventional approaches employ stainless steel cooling tubes lowered into *talha* to reduce fermentation temperatures to preserve fruit freshness and aromatics. *Talha* are not drained from the bottom; instead a hose is lowered in from the top and wine pumped out into stainless steel tanks.

Mançanita sees the point of skin contact as countering the potentially harmful effect of too much oxygen ingress while in *talha*. Too little skin contact and the wine oxidizes quickly, too much and it becomes too tannic. Managing this delicate balance requires a careful watch over the wine after fermentation to determine precisely when to remove the wine from *talha* and grape skins. Here is where Mançanita disagrees with Vinho de Talha DOC's requirement to keep wine on skins in *talha* for 2-3 months until St. Martin's Day. Rather than a rigid period applied to all wine, regardless of how individual grapes grew within a season, his approach requires more flexible timing to obtain the optimal results from the interaction between grape, their skins and the *talha*.

For example, Mançanita followed very different practical approaches in 2019, a very hot vintage, compared to 2018's cool, late harvest or the earlier picked harvest of 2017. Obviously, the acidity and ripeness levels and skin thicknesses were very different in each year.

Mançanita makes a convincing argument for his case based on historic practices. He believes 'there's a conflict between [living] memory and [more distant] history' as per the current DOC rules requiring skin contact until St. Martin's Day. He reckons how *talha* were used in the past were probably much more liberal (see section on purity).

Regardless of differences in viewpoints concerning this subject, there is enough room for both *talha* approaches to co-exist. It's pretty clear Mançanita doesn't aim to change the DOC rules and is perfectly content to go his own way making the kind of wine he wants to make using *talha* the way they suit him.

Tasting his hybrid *talha*-made white wines back to 2011 it is remarkable that all are still relatively fresh and lively for their age.

The wines

Fitapreta Signature Branco de Talha 2019 12.5%. A blend of Roupeiro and Antao Vaz. Nice bright, lively yellow color. Interesting mix of savory, mineral and slightly buttery aromas. Finely textured and slick in the mouth with a buttered popcorn/roasted nut taste to fruit and firm, slightly sharpish acidity. Almost a Chablis feel to it. Airing fleshes out texture and adds an interesting pine needle spiciness. Super reductive winemaking style, tightly knit, interesting wine with good length. Quite pure. Low alcohol for such a hot year! 89/100

Fitapreta Signature Branco de Talha 2018 12.5%. Blend of Roupeiro and Antao Vaz. No skin contact during ferment, then kept in *talha* for a month or two, removed to stainless steel tanks to mature for a year. Darker yellow. Smells of lanolin initially. Fuller richer texture than 2019, with mineral oil flavors, balanced by juicy acidity. A gastronomic style, very savory with a mineral saltiness. 87

Fitapreta Signature Branco da Talha 2017 12.5%. Blend of Roupeiro and Antao Vaz. Hints of lanolin and mineral oil aromas. A fine bodied, tightly knit wine with sweet tart lemony acidity. Clean and minerally. Low alcohol for such a hot year!

Fitapreta Signature Branco da Talha 2015 12.5%. Blend of Roupeiro and Antao Vaz. Offers a mix of green tea-like and mineral aromas. Full bodied in the mouth, textures laced mineral and roasted nut flavors.

Fitapreta Signature Branco da Talha 2011 13.5%. Blend of Roupeiro and Antao Vaz. From a ripe year, that wasn't overly hot. Lovely, indescribably complex aromas. With just a few hints of toasted notes and corn husk notes, covering subtle matured fruit in background. Quite complex in the mouth. The wine reminded me somewhat of those positive toasted characters found on 10-20 year old Australian rieslings from Eden Valley.

Fitapreta O Tinto Pote de Barro 2016 12.5%. From a 35-year-old field-blend dominated by Trincadeira. Intriguingly complex mix of spicy dried red and black fruit aromas. Leads with a silky smooth texture, that wells up with juicy red fruits mid-palate. Nice flavor length. 89

Chapter 17
Gerações da Talha

Sub-region: Vidigueira
Address: Rua de Lisboa 29A, 7960-432 Vila de Frades, Portugal
Winemaker: Teresa Caeiro
Phone: (+351 967566930)
Website: https://geracoesdatalha.com/
General Information:
Association of Vinho de Talha Producers (APVT)

It turned out to be one of those special days. I had an appointment in Vila de Frades to meet a young winemaker I hadn't previously met; Teresa Caeiro, the driving force in a 'new' adega, Gerações da Talha.

Teresa Caiero and her daughter

Upon arrival, I was elated to find that she was the grand-daughter of Professor Arlindo Ruivo, one of Alentejo's great fonts of knowledge concerning traditional *talha* practices. Crucially, she had just taken over his magnificent old adega, and was in the process of renovating one of my favorite wineries on earth.

I caught her in the midst of the first throes of a very busy harvest, with her weeks-old baby daughter in her arms, and her mother on a ladder beside them, filling a *talha* with freshly crushed grapes. Suddenly in walked the Professor himself, still lending an experienced hand and offering advice at *vendimia*. Thus the new name was explained: Gerações da Talha. Here they were, four generations - *gerações* - of a dynastic *talha* winemaking family, working together to bridge the distant past and carry it into a bright future.

Professor Arlindo Ruivo

This was great news for me. During our many meetings over the previous decade, Professor Arlindo had provided a key to my understanding of *talha*, sharing his insight, experience and deep memories of those who had come before him. Worryingly, the last time we met he was clearly tired and probably nearing the end of his semi-retirement. For many years he had been holding out the baton, always teaching and helping wherever he could, patiently waiting for someone to carry on the *talha* tradition. My fear was that the old adega might close before my next visit. Little did I know that his granddaughter was ready and waiting to carry on.

In the early-to-mid-20th century the Ruivo family's adega produced around 30,000 liters of wine, made mostly from white Antão Vaz grapes and sold in small barrels to restaurants and shops throughout the Beja region. But during the last years of the Professor's semi-retirement, production had dwindled down to just a couple of *talha* filled with enough wine for friends and family.

Now, the once densely cluttered adega - every inch a living museum devoted to the evolution of *talha* technological practices - had been cleared out. Newly freshened up with brilliant white paint, it was in the process of having its 40 old *talha* placed back into position and readied for action again. Teresa's plans are to rebuild production levels quickly to 10,000 liters and then steadily upwards from there, aiming for what the family was producing in the mid-20th century.

Purpose-built in the 17th century, the chapel-like adega is a wonderful series of Gothic arched rooms echoing those of the chapel in nearby Vila Romana de São Cucufate. Thick-walled, quiet and cool...quite a calming space actually. In the past it was a magical Aladdin's Cave of *talhas* and associated wine-making paraphernalia. I had marveled at everything the Professor had managed to cram into every nook and cranny of what had been a carefully cluttered, rust- and dust-filled cellar. Back then, I could point at anything and Professor A would have a lengthy explanation for its use and/or disuse.

Teresa assured me the treasure trove of former contents would be restored to their rightful place in the newly refurbished building.

Drawing from the best of all worlds in terms of learning her trade, Teresa studied geology at university in Lisbon, a useful background for understanding her vineyards. After that she formally studied winemaking at Evora University, grounding herself in modern practice. Perhaps most importantly, since early childhood she has worked alongside her grandfather, learning *talha* practices first hand. Knowledge that isn't taught at university... as yet.

Although technically trained, Teresa is intent on making *talha* wine as naturally and authentically as it was the past.

Her grapes are picked at perfect acidity levels, generally in late August, and go through a natural fermentation on their own yeast in *talha*. She gathers four varieties of whites, grown in separate vineyards, then co-ferments them together all in one day. The reds, Alfrocheiro, Trincadeira, Tinta Roriz, Moreto, Tinta Grossa are grown together in an old mixed 'field blend' vineyard, again co-fermented and brought in on a single day.

Both reds and whites follow the normal Vinho de Talha DOC practice of maintaining skin, seed, stem and lees contact until the official opening on St. Martin's day. Thereafter, whites are bottled in December and reds in January.

Her *talha* are lined with a traditional *pés* blend, using a local 50/50 mix of pure beeswax and pine resin. She noted that a *mãe* (the mother) takes up about a third of the *talha*'s volume, so only around 700 liters of wine are possible from each 1000-1100 liter *talha*. The 2021 vintage was on track to produce around 10,000 liters.

It is exciting to see a young person, so full of energy, re-vitalizing the old adega and carrying on where her grandfather left off. It is a fitting tribute to one of the leading lights of *talha* wine, whose life stretched back directly to a time when *talha* culture was thriving, a period when not only were there large producers supplying major cities with wine, but almost every village household had a small *talha* to serve the family over the year.

The Ruivo family carries *talha* on into the future.

The wines

Natalha Vinho de Talha Branco 2020 13% Vinho de Talha DOC. This ultra clean, full-bodied white wine is held together with very tight acidity and very fine skin tannins. Well-balanced, clean and quite minerally.

Farrapo Vinho de Talha Tinto 2020 13.5% Vinho de Talha DOC. *Farrapo* means old cloaks, alluding to those worn by monks associated with Vila de Frades, which was known as the 'village of monks.' Further back in time, there's a direct association with the nearby monks of Saõ Cucufate. It is a fruity style with red fruit characters and nicely lifted aromas and a touch of leather for interest. Still fresh, broadly fruited and mouth filling with a nicely tight bite of grippy tannins. This wine should last a long time. Although the vintage was 2 weeks earlier locally in 2020, it still managed to produce well ripened, rather than overly ripe fruit: Alfrocheiro, Trincadeira, Tinta Roriz, Moreto, Tinta Grossa.

Gerações da Talha 'Professor Arlindo' 2019 14% Vinho de Talha DOC. This is a special homage to Teresa's grandfather which was served on his birthday. It is kept for four months on 'mother' (skins, yeast lees and stems) then removed to another *talha* for a further 9 month's maturation before bottling. A field blend mix of Alfrocheiro, Trincadeira, Tinta Roriz, Moreto, Tinta Grossa, co-fermented. This is a big, rich, full-bodied wine with roasted red and blackfruit characters.

Chapter 18
Honrado & Pais das Uvas

Sub-region: Vidigueira
Honrado Vineyards & Cellar Vinaria Antiqua
Address: Rua General Humberto Delgado 17, Vila de Frades, Vidigueira 7960-446 Portugal
Managing Director & Co-Founder: Ruben Honrado
Phone & Whatsapp: +351 911 524 478
Email: info@honrado.pt
Website: https://www.honrado.pt/
General Information:
Association of Vinho de Talha Producers (APVT)
Talhas: 21 (16 large, 5 small)

País das Uvas Restaurant
Address: Rua General Humberto Delgado 19, Vila de Frades, Vidigueira 7960-446 Portugal
Phone: +351 284 441 023
Talhas: 15 (11 large, 4 medium)

Pais das Uvas is an institution. Very much a warm and welcoming institution, where people come to eat authentic local food and drink pitchers of fresh, home-made wine tapped straight from its impressive row of giant *talhas* - several of which are thoroughly scrawled from top to bottom with the names of many of Portugal's most famous, near-famous and infamous. And a few from around the world too.

Located in the beating heart of *talha* culture, Vila de Frades, Pais das Uvas differs from Alentejo's other surviving bastion of *talha*-based restaurants, Cuba's larger, grander Monte Pedral restaurant, because of its welcomingly intimate 'mom and pop' atmosphere.

Very much an extended family affair, after converting an existing 'taberna' into a *talha*-driven restaurant 20 years ago, father, António Honrado, and mother, Jacinta Penas, now run the restaurant on a daily basis, with dad making the wine. Grannies, Francisca Belbute and Amélia Caetano, refuse to completely retire and still lend a hand with the cooking on busy days. And sons Ruben and Pedro have been helping out from an early age.

Pais das Uvas is in the midst of generational rebirth. In 2006 the family purchased the bankrupt cafe next door, intent on expansion. After Ruben finished university in 2016, a decision was made to produce branded bottled wine, plant a vineyard on unused land and build a modern design winery in the new next door space. He and his brother Pedro would handle business and marketing development of the new winery.

The aim was to overcome the perennial problem with *talha* restaurants; making wine stretch through the year. Alongside the danger of some pots turning into vinegar, in older days *talha* wine was nearly all gone by February and indeed most was drunk up before December. In more modern times, better hygiene and bottling have allowed Pais das Uvas to extend to the next season, but low volumes remained a problem.

During the process of ripping out walls and floors of what was a very tackily decorated coffee shop, they uncovered Romanesque arches suggesting the building was much older than they thought. Digging ever deeper below, at 80cm they discovered an underfloor with a central drainage well of the type designed to capture lost wine from exploding *talha*. Unbeknownst to them, they had actually purchased an old adega where they intended to build a new one.

After further research, they found documentation that proved that there had been four large adegas on their street in the 1830s and two were in the space they occupied now. Thereafter the space housed a sequence of adegas and *tabernas* until in 2005 it eventually failed, serving only coffee. Which just goes to show you...

Cellar Vinaria Antiqua

Exactly how old the building is remains anyone's guess, but archaeologists suggest it could be from the 1600s, and being close to a church implies it may have been part of the early village complex. Regardless, what is interesting is the materials used and construction style would easily slot into Saõ Cucufate's Roman era complex without being noticed. Newly renamed Adega-Museu Cella Vinaria Antiqua, this fascinating old building now functions as much as an education center as an adega.

Continuing the spiritual link to the past, the Honrado family have planted a new six-hectare vineyard (Touriga Nacional, Alicante Bouchet, Trincadeira, Aragonez, Antão Vaz, Arinto, Verdelho and Roupeiro) on unused land bordering Saõ Cucufate, bringing Roman terroir back into production again.

Currently, Honrado produces 20,000 bottles of Vinho de Talha DOC made in 36 *talhas*. António continues as main winemaker with consultant Paulo Laureano providing technical support. After the restaurant's fresh *talha* supply runs dry, the basic bottled range carries on serving customers. The best *talha* from each year is bottled as 'Premium', which usually wins a gold medal at the local *talha* wine competition. They also produce a limited volume super Premium, which is bottled exclusively for Rolls Royce and Bentley Club members.

An afterthought...

My last meeting with Ruben followed the 2021 St. Martin's Day festivities where I had enjoyed an intimate 'pub crawl' of small scale, family produced *talha* wines the night before. He took me aside and reflected on the energy behind the current *talha* revival. 'Something new is going on here, that's just changed in the last few months.'

Speaking of the younger people driving XXVI Talhas (who had organized the pub crawl), Geracoes, Honrado and other newcomers, 'I think it is because the younger generation have taken over responsibility. There is a genuine spirit of sharing and cooperation. A few years ago it was everyone for themselves, but now there is a realization that people aren't competing against each other and are more powerful helping each other out, trusting the same help will be returned.'

'The older generation had more of a belief that they were superior and didn't need or want others' help... Now if I have too many conflicting appointments I'll send my clients off to my neighbors to see what they produce. I'm not competing with them, we help each other, because we all share the same culture. We help ourselves by helping each other out.'

The parting of the olive oil…Ruben Honrado working his magic

White wines

Honrado Branco Vinho de Talha DOC 2021 13% Vinho de Talha DOC. This blend of Antao Vaz, Arinto, Perrum and Diagalves offers up spicy aniseed and applesauce aromas, followed with quince, peach and apricot-like flavors. Textures round out nicely with just enough skin tannins and acidity to balance the wine. Deep yellow in color. A gastronomic style, able to cut through any food served at the restaurant. A classic everyday *talha* table wine, 11 months on from birth it's still able to bridge the gap until the next St. Martin's Day. 88/100

Honrado Premium Branco Vinho de Talha DOC 2020 13% This blend of Antao Vaz, Arinto, Perrum and Fernão Pires has a deep golden yellow color. Mineral based aromas offer hints of aniseed and green veggie. Full bodied, with condensed, savory flavored fruits, all this nicely tempered by firm acidity. 90

Honrado Branco Vinho de Talha DOC 2017 From an old mixed vineyard of Antão Vaz, Roupeiro and many other vines. Honrado's consultant winemaker, Paulo Laureano showed me this wine in 2018, saying 'it was a true wine from *talha*.' Opening with neutral aromas, these developed subtle spiced honeyed notes. Slightly honeyed with some viscosity middle-mouth, it carried on with interesting visceral textures from skin tannins, underpinned by acidity. Further airing showed pear skin and peach pit aromas/flavors developing. Overall a well rounded, clean finishing wine. Laureano explained that in the past these wines were served in small water glasses, drunk at room temp, and not with food, intended as something more to share in conversation with friends.

Red Wines

Honrado Tinto Vinho de Talha DOC 2021 14% A blend of Alfrocheiro, Aragonez, Trincadeira and Alicante Bouchet. Interesting mix of red fruit, plum and mineral aromas, followed by savory, mouthcoating red fruits with good length and fine grippy tannins to balance. A perfect dinner wine for cutting through hearty Alentejo food. 89

Honrado Premium Tinto Vinho de Talha DOC 2021 15% A blend of Tinta Grossa, Aragonez, Trincadeira and Alfrocheiro. Opens with black fruit and mineral aromas. A relatively subtle, restrained nose, that develops vanilla notes after airing. A mix of black and red fruit flavors in the mouth showing good concentration and depth, underpinned and driven forward with fine, but firm, tannins. The wine has seen two months maturation in oak barrels, dressing it with vanilla aromas and flavors. 92

Honrado Tinto Vinho de Talha DOC 2019 14.5% A serviceable table wine, showing its hot year's season: spirity, roasted black and red fruit aromas. Tasting of dark dense berry fruits with chewy, rustic tannins. 86/100

Honrado Premium Tinto Vinho de Talha DOC 2019 15.5% From their best amphora of the vintage. Limited bottling that changes yearly: 920 bottles, but sometimes 800 or 1500. From a super hot vintage, it's surprisingly less stewy, spirity, cleaner, and more sharply focused than the baseline 2019 Vinho de Talha DOC. Tons of dried blackfruit characters with a slick, alcohol laden texture, good length, relatively fine tannins. Continuous, seamless. Nice wine. 2019 was very hot, luckily 2020 is down to more normal 13.5%. Tasted 9.21

Honrado Premium Tinto 2019 15.5% Retasted on 3.11.21 From super hot 2019, but wears its alcohol well. A touch spirity, with roasted black fruit characters, seamless texture, good length and fine tannins. 93

Honrado Premium Tinto 2019 15.5% Retasted on 24.12.21 An amalgamation of stewed/cooked black fruit aromas, surprisingly less spirited, this bottle. Also different in the mouth, very port-like, sweetly ripe fruit characters with hot, alcohol infused texture. Light tannins and low acidity make it a soft finishing wine. Full and thick bodied, it proved ideal for Christmas Eve accompanying hard cheese and spicy, heavy bodied, traditional British desserts; fruit mince pie, figgy, treacle & sticky puddings, Xmas cake, etc. With airing aromas become more port-like. Great length. Like a dry port. 96

Honrado Premium Tinto 2017 14% Vinho de Talha DOC A remarkably balanced wine from another, slightly less, hot vintage. Made from Aragonez, Alicante Bouchet and very local Tinta Grossa grapes. Opens with a mix of mineral, dried black fruit aromas, playing out in the mouth with a shift towards more red fruit flavors. Great acidity and a finer, lighter texture than expected at 14 degrees Alcohol. Great length of flavor. This wine should evolve and survive a few decades more into the future, but a terrific drink now. With airing it expands into black cherry flavors, ever more concentration and really long after flavors. 96

Palhete

Honrado Palhete 2022 12% Bottled on St Martins Day, this is an ultra-fresh mixture of Antao Vaz, Viosinho, Arinto and a 5% tinting of Trincadeira. Offering lovely strawberry characters delivered through a smooth texture underpinned by softish acidity. A nice easy drinking glugger. 86

Chapter 19
Jose de Sousa

Sub-region: Reguengos
Address: Adega José de Sousa Rosado Fernandes, R. de Mourão, 1 7200-291 Reguengos de Monsaraz, 38°25'29.57"N | 7°31'47.06"W
Owners and parent company: José Maria da Fonseca
Winemakers: Domingo Soares Franco and Paulo Amaral
Email: josedesousa@jmfonseca.pt
Phone: +351 918 269 569
Website: https://www.jmf.pt/index.php?id=212
General information: José de Sousa Rosado Fernandes Winery - The Essence of a Wine Family - Winetourism - José Maria da Fonseca (jmf.pt)

If the dozens of small family-run adegas and tavernas serve as the chapels and parish churches keeping *talha* tradition alive and villagers in everyday wine, then José de Sousa is *talha* culture's cathedral.

Jose de Sousa Cathedral of *Talha*

Echoing Villa Romana de S. Cucufate's gothic arched ceilings, cool, dark, atmospheric subterranean cellar and neat rows of 114 large *talha*, it certainly looks the part.

But there is a spiritual connection here as well. Just as the soul of home-made *talha* wine was nearly snuffed out in the late 20th century, José de Sousa's direct link back to large scale Roman production came dangerously close to extinction in the 1980s.

What most of us don't realize in the 2020s is that back in 1986, outside of Georgia and a handful of villagers in Alentejo, virtually no one was making wine in clay pots. Hardly anyone outside of these areas even knew it was possible. This was a good fifteen years before the first Italian winemakers started playing around with this ancient technology that helped establish the modern 'amphora' movement. And it was twenty-five years before Alentejo established its Vinho de Talha DOC rules.

The story of José de Sousa's resurrection is central to the modern revival of *talha* winemaking (see historical overview section). Established on the outskirts of Reguengos de Monsaraz in 1878, Casa Agrícola José de Sousa Rosado Fernandes (with nearby vineyards at Herdade do Monte da Ribeira) was a massive wine making factory containing around 120 large (1500+ liter) *talhas* with production capacity well over 100,000 bottles. Among the most venerated of Alentejo's grand old 19th century wine producers, Mouchao, Tapata do Chaves, Carmo (now Dona Maria), only Jose de Sousa has made *talha* wine continuously into the present era.

Many of its red wines are legendary. Some of them are still drinking remarkably well going back to the 1940s. These remain the oldest surviving clay pot-produced wines anywhere in the world today. This is a testament to both the winery and the technology that produced them.

After the winery's golden era (1940–60s), wine making at José de Sousa lost its way in the 1970s. The last generation of this great *talha* wine business had died and winemaking was turned over to consultants with little practical knowledge of *talha* winemaking. Quality and volumes dwindled to their lowest level. After the 1974 revolution, the vineyards were confiscated by communists and run into the ground for lack of proper care. Then in 1984 three workers died of carbon dioxide asphyxiation, and production ground to a halt.

A revival of fortunes came after José Maria da Fonseca, one of Portugal's leading progressive producers, purchased José de Sousa in 1986. At that point the winery was in a ruinous state with only 20 or so *talha* still surviving, many of those cracked or stapled back together.

Part of the original negotiating team, Fonseca's University of Davis-trained chief winemaker, Domingos Soares Franco, had a deep respect for José de Sousa's *talha* production, old wines and old vine, Grand Noir-dominant vineyards. If Franco hadn't been both a family member and chairman of the board - not to mention, a visionary - José de Sousa probably wouldn't have been restored to its former glory.

There were several major problems that needed solutions. No-one made *talha* anymore after factory production collapsed in the 1920s, so replacement of *talha* was an issue. Similarly, the cellar's old 3000-5000 liter chestnut barrels were too leaky or dirty to use. These also weren't being made at the time, so couldn't be replaced. And crucially, there were no records or manuals concerning how *talha* wine had been made at José de Sousa, nor did the current cellarmen have any connection with past practices. Franco - schooled in the most up-to-date winemaking technology and techniques - had to puzzle it all out for himself.

The first tasks were cleaning up the two old stone *lagars*, clearing out broken barrels from the cellar and weeding out all the leaky pots. Franco then started buying up all the *talha* he could find for sale at antique shops and gardening stores or hanging around as lawn decorations and architectural features. Eventually the old 120 quorum was restored. He also located the old head winemaker/cellarman from the great 1950-60 era, who proved instrumental in helping him understand how they made *talha* wine in the past. As importantly, he learned to approach *talhas* on their own terms, not from a modern perspective. It was, to say the least, a very steep learning curve.

But by the 1990s, José de Sousa was back on track, producing well-made, fresh, clean, enjoyable wine again. They also had reacquired the old vineyard planted in 1952 at Herdade do Monte da Ribeira and restored it to its former glory. The next phase was to work toward reproducing the great 'Rosado Fernandes' wines of the past.

Domingos Soares Franco inspecting an exploded talha

José de Sousa's large-scale production differed from small *talha* production in two significant ways. The first was the large, rectangular stone *lagars* that allowed grapes to be gently crushed by foot before being drained into *talha* below.

The second were dozens of wooden 3000-5000 liter casks (*foudres*) which reduced oxidation and allowed *talha* wine to be aged for long periods before bottling. Lacking access to these large old chestnut *foudres*, Franco turned to standard 225-liter new French oak barrels instead.

The first of Fonseca's new *talha* style wine, called Mayor, was bottled in 1994. This was a 'reserve' blend of Grand Noir (55%), Trincadeira (35%) and Aragonês (10%) that was foot trodden in *lagars* with 30% stems added to the *talha*. Recalling that the old cellarmaster had told Franco they used *lagars* and *talha* in tandem, he fermented half the grapes in *talha* and kept half in *lagar* to ferment. After fermentation, both lots were blended together in November or December and transferred to French oak barrels for nine months of ageing.

Eventually an elevated 'grand reserve' brand was added in 2007. This was produced only in the best vintages and called 'J'. Here the grape blend changed to Grand Noir (55%), Touriga Francesa (30%) and Touriga Nacional (15%). Importantly, they were sourced exclusively from the old vine, mixed variety 'José de Sousa Vineyard' planted in 1952/53, a vineyard that had replanted vines directly from an older vineyard which had supplied the great Jose de Sousa wines of the 1940s. Another major difference with Major is that 'J' was fermented only in *talha* and then was aged in French oak barriques for 9 months.

Over time Franco realized he still hadn't cracked the classic 'Rosado Fernandes' styles made in the 1940s, 50s and 60s. French oak's dominant characters were overshadowing the transparency of *talha*-fermented fruit. This begged for much more neutral, less intrusive, large chestnut casks.

Chestnut cask at Jose de Sousa

The culmination of a decades-long search to recreate one of *talha*'s greatest wines, Puro Tinto, appeared in 2015. José de Sousa's first wine to gain Vinho de Talha DOC certification, it was made along the lines of 'J', but with two subtle changes. The grape blend was tweaked slightly with addition of Moreto, an old Alentejo, *talha*-associated, variety. This lightened and freshened up the blend. More significantly, 'J's 'modern style' French oak maturation was replaced by maturation in 600-liter chestnut casks.

One cannot over-stress how radical it was in the 1980s for José Maria da Fonseca to throw its energy and treasure behind such a crazy concept as making wine in ancient clay pots. This was an ultra-modern wine company selling its products all over the world to consumers with expectations of squeaky clean, fruit filled, easy-to-appreciate wine.

Much of their task has involved teaching people throughout the world that old technology isn't primitive technology, but one capable of making a distinctive style in its own right. Rather than reproduce a wine for daily consumption, they chose instead to make serious, labor-intensive wine that would command the highest price and the respect that *talha* wine deserved.

After more than thirty years of championing *talha* wine, few realize that Jose de Sousa remains the oldest producer of *talha* wine in the world. It's not something they mention, although they could easily brag about it. They may also be the longest-running producer of wine made in clay pots anywhere in the world as well. All this says more than enough about what they've accomplished (or maybe...Enough said).

The wines

The wines below are from José de Sousa's historical 'golden era' (1940–65), rediscovery-revival period (1986-1994), modern hybrid *talha* Major and J (1994-present) and the modern 'Puro' Vinho de Talha DOC range (2015-present)

Historical wines: José de Sousa Rosado Fernandes 1940-1965

José de Sousa Rosado Fernandes 1940 14.6%. Staggeringly fresh and lively for a 75-year-old. Aromas are in a dried, black-fruit spectrum, complex and expansive, with base notes of licorice, caramel, and unsweetened cocoa, further highlighted with spice and floral characters. Well-rounded and velvety in the mouth, more than amply fruited for its age, its textures outlined by lovely polymerized tannins and relatively low acidity. It finished long, with just a touch of dryness. A wine for contemplation and respect, rather than scoring. But if one has to score it: 99/100 (Tasted 2014)

José de Sousa Rosado Fernandes 1940 14.6%. 2nd tasting Aug 2021 at Fialho, Evora. For an 81-year-old wine, it is still holding well and offering a mix of savory characters above. It opened up, markedly improving, over the course of a two hour dinner. What was impressive was how a 14.6% wine didn't show overt alcohol, especially in light of its age and more delicate condition. Acidity holding in balance with fruit. A remarkable testament to *talha*-made wine. (Tasted 2021) 96

[Franco told me the 1940s were uniquely bottled in transparent American whiskey bottles because they were the only bottles available during the war. All others used green glass.]

José de Sousa Rosado Fernandes 1945. Compared to the 1940, this is fresher on the nose, with more herbal high tones, higher acidity, and sappier, more savory fruit notes. Great length. (Tasted 2014) 94

José de Sousa Rosado Fernandes 1953. Initially more oxidative, with chocolate/coffee aromas, full-bodied and sappy. With airing, it freshens up, developing spicy high tones. Packed with fruits, fleshy textures, and firm tannins. (Tasted 2014) 96

José de Sousa Rosado Fernandes Tinto Velho 1961. Foot-trodden, then to *talha*, matured in concrete. Virtually no browning here. Remarkably fresh, lifted aromas in a very complete, well-balanced nose: a mix of dried herbs, savory red-plum aromas, and the faintest hint of tar. Creamy smooth on entry, cool in the mouth, with firm, ripe stem tannins. Structured firmly, in the best sense, with complex flavors right through the finish. Excellent wine, at its peak of perfection. (Tasted 2014) 98

José de Sousa Rosado Fernandes 1964. Opens with pronounced dark-chocolate aromas, then follows with fresh, clean, lively red fruits, leaning toward dried cherries. Palate weight is nicely balanced, with fresh acidity. Good length. Excellent wine. (Tasted 2014) 94

José de Sousa Rosado Fernandes 1965. What promises to be a big complex nose crimped down with probable low-level cork taint, TCA confirmed by astringency on the palate. Sadly, this is meant to be one of Grand Noir's finest vintages. (Tasted 2014) not scored

Early revival period 1986-1994

José de Sousa Garrafeira 1990. The first vintage that was only from the oldest mixed vineyard. Broad, fleshy, red-fruited, with spirity lift, the acidity more prominent than the tannins. From the old mixed variety 'José de Sousa Vineyard' planted in 1952/53 (Tasted 2014) 88

Jose de Sousa Garrafeira 1991 12.5%. Fruitier, more floral than the 1990, adding a roasted red-fruit core. Nice, fine, tart-cherry bitterness and good length. From the old mixed variety 'José de Sousa Vineyard' planted in 1952/53 (Tasted 2014) 90

Mayor, first modern hybrid style: 1994-present

Approximate blend Grand Noir (55%), Trincadeira (35%), Aragonês (10%). Foot trodden in *lagars* with 30% stems added to *talha* at fermentation. A hybrid 50/50 *talha/lagar* fermentation, thereafter transferred in November or December to oak barrels for 9 months. Originally from 1.8h vineyard, but recent vineyards also draw from other vineyards. 7-8.800 liters = 9,300-12,000 bottles.

José de Sousa 1994 Mayor 13%. The first year of the elevated Mayor branding. A complex mix of floral, cocoa, and dried-cherry aromas. Densely fruited on the palate, with firm, juicy, mouth-puckering acidity. Good length on the finish. (Tasted 2014) 89

José de Sousa Mayor 1997. A beautifully balanced wine from a classic year that dances across one's nose and palate. Nutty aromas are backgrounded with fresh floral and dark cocoa notes. Fresh red-fruit juiciness spins through a seamless texture and a long finish. (Tasted 2014) 96

José de Sousa Mayor 1999 13.5%. Spirity on the nose, with fruits leaning in over ripe, date/raisin and cocoa spectrum. Domingos sees this as a more classic 1940s style. Lots of fruit, concentration, firmly structured. For long-term drinking. (Tasted 2014) 90

José de Sousa Mayor 2001 14.3%. A big powerful wine, packed with complex chocolate, dried-fruit, and floral characters, concentrated without being heavy. Seamless texture, underpinned by multilayered tannic/acid structure. Excellent balance for its alcohol. (Tasted 2014) 96

José de Sousa Mayor 2004 14.9%. From a very hot season. Dried bitter red-cherry aromas, dried-out, astringent tannins, hollow-bodied from vine stress? May come right in time. (Tasted 2014) 85

José de Sousa Mayor 2007 13%. Beautifully balanced nose: broadly floral, fresh, and spicy. Full-bodied and richly concentrated; all this held in check by firm tannins and grippy acids.(Tasted 2014) 90

José de Sousa Mayor 2009 14%. Full-bodied and highly concentrated, and yet relatively elegant and finely structured. It offers great fruit depth, integration, and an exceptionally long, melt-away finish. For cellaring. (Tasted 2014) 99

José de Sousa Mayor 2012. Date, fig, and dried black-fruit aromas, with hints of cocoa and caramel. Voluptuous texture and expansive fruit, struck through by fine tannins. (Tasted 2014) 89

Jose de Sousa Mayor 2014 14%. A hybrid style, this isn't pure Vinho de Talha DOC, but 50% *talha*-produced. Grand Noir 58, Trincadeira 30%, Aragonez from Reguengos de Monsaraz. 12% fermented in *talha,* then aged for 9 months in 30% French Oak casks. Vanilla oak aromas and tannins are quite present and cover red fruits. Needs a lot more time to integrate. From a cooler moderate vintage that has less fruit to amass against barrique influence. 2 hours later, oak character becomes integrated into savory dried red fruits, felt now more than smelled or tasted. Fruit fleshing out to meet strong oaking, I suspect. Quite persistent flavors. (Tasted 2019) 89

Jose de Sousa Mayor 2017. A blend of 60% Grand Noir, Trincadeira 20%, Aragonez 20%. 3000 liters. Interesting hybrid with ½ only fermented 1 week in *talha* and ½ fermented in *lagars,* then sent to barrels. Creamy smooth entry and continuous texture, then fine tannins and firm acidity. Spicy blackfruit, focused, fine elegant texture with great refreshing acidity and length. And fruit on finish. 94

Establishment of José de Sousa J Super Premium

(*talha*-made plus French oak)

Only produced in best vintages. Foot trodden in *lagars*, then fermented in *talha* and aged in French oak barriques for 9 months. Generally a blend around Grand Noir (55%), Touriga Francesa (30%), Touriga Nacional (15%). Exclusively from the old mixed variety 'José de Sousa Vineyard' planted in 1952/53. Approximately 2500l = 3500 bottles.

José de Sousa J 2007. Dark fruit aromas, fresh blackberry, cocoa and coffee flavors, slick in the mouth; all this underpinned by fine, firm, full-mouth tannins and pert, juicy acidity. Nice clean finish. From old, mixed vine 'José de Sousa Vineyard' planted in 1952/53 (Tasted 2014) 89

José de Sousa J 2009 13%. Leading with vanilla, mocha, and red-fruit aromas. A fantastic mouthfeel, with perfectly balanced fruit weight. Neatly structured, well-integrated tannins traverse ultra-long, finely tapered finish. From the old mixed variety 'José de Sousa Vineyard' planted in 1952/53. (Tasted 2014) 99

José de Sousa J 2011 13.5%. A very smooth wine, with a beautifully integrated, complex nose: hints of spice, cedar, blueberry, black fruits, dates, figs, and dried straw. Nicely concentrated, complex, finely focused flavors that hang on to the tongue tip for minutes. From the old mixed variety 'José de Sousa Vineyard' planted in 1952/53 (Tasted 2014) 96

Jose de Sousa 'J' 2014 14%. A hybrid style, this isn't pure Vinho de Talha DOC. A blend of Grand Noir, Tinta Francesa, Touriga Nacional from Reguengos de Monsaraz. Fermented in *talha,* then aged for 10m French oak casks. Licorice/aniseed oak notes side-by-side with dried black fruit aromas and flavors. Excellent fruit dept throughout with firm oak tannins extending to and after finish. Tannins coat lips. For a 14% wine this is relatively light bodied and elegant. Needs more time in bottle to show its best. Drink 2020-2030+ After 2 hours of breathing, oakiness dissipated into more floral black fruits characters. Wine shows more finesse and elegance now, but still young and asking for more time in bottle. From the old mixed variety 'José de Sousa Vineyard' planted in 1952/53. (Tasted 2019) 96

Puro Vinho de Talha DOC: 2015-present

(a return to Jose de Sousa's Rosado Fernandes traditional historical style)

Puro Tinto follows the path begun by 'J' using the same old vineyard, the red grapes from the old mixed variety 'José de Sousa Vineyard' planted in 1952/53. It also is produced by foot treading in *lagars*, with 30% addition of stems, and 100% fermentation in *talha*. Where it significantly departs is by following Vinho de Talha DOC certification after St. Martin's Day and maturation in large 600-liter Portuguese chestnut barrels (production under 6,000 bottles).

Puro Tinto Vinho de Talha DOC

Jose de Sousa Puro Talha Tinto 2015 12.5% Vinho de Talha DOC. A classic blend of Grand Noir (50%), Trincadeira (20%), Aragonês (20%), Moreto (10%) grapes from 'José de Sousa Vineyard' planted in 1952/53. Fermented in *talha,* then aged for 14-16 months in 600-liter chestnut casks. First tasted in 2017 when young, spicy and aromatic with great purity. Concentrated, firm textures and a long, persistent finish, with pure red fruit flavors through to end. Retasted in 2019, it had matured into super-ripe, mulberry, prune, date and a mélange of dried black fruit (Grand Noir?) aromas and flavors. These roasted dried fruit characters resulting from a hot year presumably. After airing, these refocus, becoming fresher, more like dried black cherry characters. Lots of fine, firm tannins and tart cherryish acidity in the mouth driving length. The wine is a bit of a trickster because the super-ripe fruit aromas suggest a big, fat alcoholic, low acid texture, but in the mouth it shifts gears into something more linear: light-bodied and tartly juicy with great back palate length. Super-fine tannins underpin acidity. Deceptively long. A really nice wine. This was the first year of this new style and much more like the originals from the 40s than J or Mayor. (Stems from Trincadeira were used to make this wine but weren't used after because they made the wine too peppery.) Last tasted 11.2019, previously tasted 2017 & 2018. 96

Jose De Sousa Puro Talha Tinto 2017 13.5% Vinho de Talha DOC. This vintage more or less followed the formula from 2015, increasing Moreto ratio to freshen up the wine. It also traded Trincadiera for Aragonês (Tempranillo) stems for structure and spice. Still a baby, offering a spicy mix of fresh and ripe mulberry and red fruit characters, full fleshy body underpinned with long-grained, super-fine tannins and juicy finish. Quite elegant and remarkably low alcohol from a hot year and hot region! Bottled in October 2021. Excellent all round and reminiscent of the Rosado Fernandes wines of the past. Grapes are from 'José de Sousa Vineyard' planted in 1952/53. Retasted 11.22. Although still juicy, the wine has taken on additional darker, dried fruit and date characters, while still retaining tons of finesse. 96

Puro Branco Vinho de Talha DOC: 2016 to present

Under 1000 bottles, white grapes sourced from old mixed variety vines from 'José de Sousa Vineyard' planted in 1952/53.

Jose De Sousa Puro Talha Branco 2017 12.5% Vinho de Talha DOC. This wine, from a cooler year, spent less time aged in clay, 8months. Spicier, hints of nutty characters. Shows more acidity and is fuller bodied, with fleshier texture. Tasted one year later on St. Martins Day 2022, the wine has developed apple skin and walnut aromas. A very finely textured, even tempered, gastronomic style of wine with a degree of elegance. 90

Jose De Sousa Puro Branco Talha 2016 12% Vinho de Talha DOC. This blend of Antao Vaz, Manteudo and Diagalves spent six months on skins, blending in one part stems to give a feeling of acidity. After removing from skins it was returned to clay for 10 months covered in olive oil, then matured for a year in bottle. It wears a deep, bright, golden-orange color. Darker color deceptively implies it could be oxidized, but isn't at all. Wine has interesting Pekoe tea-like aromas and flavors, fine acidity, clean, very fine viscosity, supported by quite elegantly structured, fine skin tannins. Butterscotch aromas emerge with airing. A lot to unlock in this wine. Not a quaffer, one for contemplation, sipping over a long evening. From 'José de Sousa Vineyard' planted in 1952/53 (Tasted 11.2021) 90

Private Collection

Jose de Sousa Private Collection Sarigo 2021. A very fine, lifted elegant bouquet, with fresh, delicate green flower stem aromas. Creamy smooth texture, laced with citrus acidity, then very fine skin tannins follow to lengthen finish. Develops broader, fresher brighter florals with more air. This followed a 10-day ferment in *talha*, kept on skins for 3 weeks then sent to stainless steel tanks until bottling. Only 600 liters produced and deemed a private expression with no makeup or additions. Sarigo is an ancient, nearly extinct local variety that was planted in 1952/53 era 'José de Sousa Vineyard'. Because Sarigo is not an officially sanctioned grape variety in Alentejo's modern era, it can't be approved as a Vinho de Talha DOC wine. This unfortunate Catch 22 situation has destined this wine for a Private Collection bottling (Tasted 11.21). Retasted 11.22 it has developed buttery notes with a filled-out texture infused with ripe melon and citrus fruits. Elegantly styled it retains a fresh, clean finish. 96

Jose de Sousa Private Collection Sarigo 2022 11.5%. Franco is impressed with this grape, feeling it has a great future ahead of it primarily because it can stand both heat and sun and still deliver high acidity and lowish alcohol. The 2022, a sample direct from *talha* on St Martins Day, offers delicate fresh green stem and white flower blossom aromas accompanied by fresh crisp textures. Franco feels the grape is too delicate for a full St Martins Day maceration, so has given it a quick two week fermentation in clay, then removed it to stainless steel.

Jose de Sousa Private Collection Pote Grande Noir 2018. This rare 100% Grande Noir wine spends three years in clay pots. It differs from the Puro range highlighting Grande Noir's herbal, lifted florals and mulberry fruit characters. Richly textured in the mouth, with fresh black fruits, and crunch acidity. Still unreleased, it's one to watch out for.

Chapter 20
Adega Marel

Sub-region: Granja-Amareleja
Address: Soc. Vitivinícola Courela dos Aleixos, Lda.
EN 385, km 21, 7885-012 Amareleja, Portugal
Owners/winemakers: Tiago Macena, David Morgado, Raúl Moreno-Yague
Email: adega@adegamarel.pt
Website: www.adegamarel.pt

A relatively new player, founded in 2018, Adega Marel is a cooperative venture driven by Dao-based winemaker Tiago Macena and Alentejo-based marketer/manager David Morgado, whose family own the original adega. More recently Seville-based winemaker Raúl Moreno-Yague has joined forces with them in a couple of interesting experimental wines.

Tiago Macena

Youthful and dynamic, the project is notable for its mix of traditional and modern winemaking techniques and cross-border collaboration. It is the first instance I know of where Spanish and Portuguese have explored winemaking together.

Tiago Macena has been deeply involved in Portugal's Dao wine region for years, having made wine for major players Casa de Santar and Boas Quintas as well as others in Douro, Bairrada and Australia. He is also studying for the Master of Wine exam, systematically broadening his wine knowledge on a global level.

Moreno-Yague is a very much a citizen of the world, having studied viticulture and winemaking in Australia and worked in Rioja, Jerez, Burgundy, Douro, Istria, South Africa and Georgia, the origin of *qvevri* clay pot wine making. He brings an Andalusian perspective from just across the border in Jerez, having made wine in *Tinaja* clay pots, the Spanish counterpart to *talha*.

David Morgado provides the place to make the wine and, more importantly, extensive roots back into Alentejo's Granja-Amareleja subregion with family, ancestry and friends deeply woven into the fabric of the local *talha* culture.

A key figure is Morgado's grandfather, António, after whom they named their traditionally made Tonico Vinho de Talha DOC range, Tonico being António's nickname among close friends. An accomplished 'modern' winemaker, now turned apprentice, Macena warmly credits António as the first person to teach - indeed, continues to advise - him how to make traditional *talha* wine.

António's influence was the key to unlocking local *talha* culture. As they got to know António better, they also met his friends, who proudly showed them their vineyards and their *talha* in turn. Gradually this community came to accept the newer generation and became a natural source of fruit, *talhas* and knowledge as the project grew in size and depth over time.

The adega owns 14 hectares of vines, all traditional local varieties, some in mixed field blends and others more focused on a single variety or two. These are in several smaller parcels on different soil types, each named after the local families or old friends they bought them from. Two of these parcels are old vineyards, and one, Pura, is very old, dating from before 1930.

Those of us outside of farming often don't realize how important the passing on of ownership and stewardship of land is to a traditional villager. Men who have devoted their life tending a small plot have a huge emotional investment in seeing it well cared for after they move on. Respectful continuity is clearly something the young team at Adega Marel value.

Originally, Adega Marel started off with three family owned *talha* and now draws wine from thirteen, all locally manufactured. Similar to vineyards, the old *talha* are nicknamed after Antonio's old friends, former owners and the *talha's* characteristics: Preta 500Kg, Cruzeiro (dated 1800) 600kg, Bancaleiro 1000Kg, Barriga Cheia (full tummy) 800 kg, Mal-Talhado 800 kg, Chico 200kg, 3 Gatos (3 cats) 300kg, Charuto (cigar shaped) 500Kg, Comissário (Policeman) 800 kg, Patrício 1400 Kg, Arnega 500 kg, Mal-Talhado 2 700 kg, Chico Açorda 650 Kg.

Adega Marel's blend of traditional *talha* and vineyards and more modern technology plays out through several wine styles. The adega's 'modern' styled wines are conventionally made from local grapes in stainless steel tanks. The Marel (a top breeding stud sheep or goat) range is focused on capturing the vineyard's character: fresh, fruit-focused and easy drinking. An evolutionary hybridized departure from this is Marel's Illustre, which ferments and then ages the wine in stainless steel until February 2021, thereafter maturing for another four months in *talha*. The clay's porosity works like an oak barrel to soften tannins.

A step up in quality from Marel, Manolito is named after David Morgado's great uncle, an extroverted, much loved character who traveled widely, promoting Amareleja wherever he went and returning with colorful stories enthusiastically shared with the folks back home. This hybrid style blends both *talha*-made and stainless steel-produced wines together, creating something fuller bodied and more complex, with savory edged fruit. It works as an introduction to *talha* wines, bridging Marel's fruit focus and the purer, more traditional textural experience of Tonico's DOC style. I found these to be really interesting wines that honestly tracked the ups and downs of vintage variation, illustrating the seasonal interaction between land and grapes and sun.

Rethinking ancient technology - outside the box - is also part of the ethos at Adega Marel. The Spanish branch of this threesome, Raúl Moreno-Yague, has brought some intriguing new ideas drawn from the outer edges of both the

New World and the Ancient World of wine. Combining Georgian techniques he learned at Okro Wines and Pheasant Tears, with squeaky clean Australian practices from university days, he invented a novel approach towards a lighter, more controlled gentle extraction in *talha*. After foot treading grapes into a paste, this was placed into mesh bags inserted into *talha* and then submerged with weights to keep it all under a liquid surface.

Pretty clever stuff. The result is more fruit intensity, less astringent tannins and more finesse, plus less oxidation and avoidance of vinegary, volatile acidity (VA). One can imagine this may also alter the convection flow inside the *talha* as well.

The technique is employed on the so far unnamed cross border collaboration between Adega Marel & Moreno-Yague, involving early picked, acid sharp Rabo de Ovelha (Sheep's tail) with old vine Antão Vaz and Roupeiro (adding structure and complexity) fermented in *talha* and thereafter aged in 100-year-old, 800-liter, Amontillado (Sherry) Chestnut Barrels. The barrels add less astringent tannins than oak, and being more porous, develop wine more quickly. Moreno-Yague observes that, "an Amontillado cask delivers layers of saltiness, 'Sotolon' and roasted nuts & seeds." I also picked up hints of interesting 'rancio' nuttiness leached out of Sherry residues in these old barrels. The style is unlike anything I've tasted from anywhere, truly something new.

All in all, this project is in the process of exploring an intriguing mix of ancient and cutting-edge practice. On one hand respectfully replicating old styles, while busily spinning out entirely new concepts of wine. Although still early days, there is promise of some pretty amazing creativity emerging.

The wines

Traditional Vinho de Talha DOC

Adega Marel Tonico Branco 2021. From a field blend vineyard, *talha*-fermented and kept on skins into January, then bottled in May. Newly released November 2022. A very well mannered wine, aromatically fresh and complete unto itself at this point in time. Smooth, slick and elegantly textured with sappy acidity and well judged, nicely integrated tannins. 90/100

Adega Marel Tonico Branco 2019 14.5% Vinho de Talha DOC Granja-Amareleja. This is an authentic white wine style commonly drunk in local taverns directly out of the pots they were made in. Captured in bottle with a couple of years of maturation, it opens with neutralish mineral and slightly honeyed, quince aromas. Plenty of acidity here, driving flavor length through a medium body with subtle mineral flavors and balancing skin tannins. 88

Adega Marel Tonoica Tinto 2021. This 100% Moreto is kept on skins into January, then shifted to stainless steel tanks and bottled in July. Packed full of lifted red cherry characters driven by fine, firm tannins. Very tightly structured wine, with a degree of finesse, edgy acidity and great flavor length. 94

Adega Marel Tonico Tinto 2020 13% Vinho de Talha DOC Granja-Amareleja. This is an authentic red wine style commonly drunk in local taverns directly out of the pots they were made in. Savory, slightly tarry red fruit aromas, dried cherry fruitiness with finely astringent tannins, in a pleasing reassuring way. Balancing acidity keeps wine fresh with decent persistence. For what should be a modest wine, it's impressive for its vinosity and length. Next day, the tarry backs off, instead offering more dried blackfruit, dates, prunes with a touch of florals. Tannins are very long and fine now. 90

Hybrid white wines

Adega Marel Manolito Branco 2020 12.5% Granja-Amareleja. Color is rich yellow on the way to amber. After a hot 2019, this blend of Diagalves and Antao Vaz dials back to a more reasonable traditional lower alcohol level and balanced acidity. Neutral, mineral aromas and flavors play out through a medium bodied wine, with fine viscosity and excellent acid balance driving flavor length. It's distinguished by persistent after flavors and super mouthfeel and weight. 94

Adega Marel Manolito Branco 2019 14% Granja-Amareleja. Dark amber colored. For a two-year-old wine from a hot year in a hot climate, pushed forward by an oxidative fermentation, it's holding its own well enough. Blending Diagalves and Antao Vaz, it offers relatively neutral mineral aromas. Texturally thick and viscous, with relatively subtle flavors and nice acidity to finish. At its peak, it probably needs drinking up. 88

Adega Marel Manolito Branco 2018 13.5% Granja-Amareleja. Light amber color. This blend of Diagalves and Antao Vaz was hard to read. Its mix of honeyed aromas and honeyed/orange marmalade flavors suggested it was on the edge of oxidation. But then it followed with really high acidity. In the end I wasn't sure it was oxidized or more the character of grapes and their state of maturation. 86

Hybrid Red wines

Adega Marel Manolito Tinto 2019 14% Granja-Amareleja. This red blend of Moreto and Trincadeira combined portions of *talha* fermented and stainless steel fermented wine, aged further in stainless steel tanks. Very closed and tight initially, 24 hours later it blossomed into quite a generous wine. Leading with spirity, roasted, dried black fruit and vanilla aromas, similar flavors followed. Given the high alcohol, it was much finer bodied than expected, with juicy acidity driving length. 88

Adega Marel Manolito Tinto 2018 13.5% Granja-Amareleja. A red blend of Moreto and Trincadeira combining portions of *talha* fermented and stainless steel fermented wine, aged further in stainless steel tanks. Lots of spice and dried herbal high-toned aromas over a baseline of berry notes. Soft and rounded, a viscous mouthfeel enfolds gentle tannins and acidity. With airing it expands into a mouthful of fresh black and red raspberry flavors and develops a surprising juiciness. 89

Adega Marel Illustre Tinto 2019 14% Granja-Amareleja. Fermented in stainless steel, then aged for four months in *talha*. Mostly mineral aromas with hints of frozen blueberries and mulberries. Sweet, brambly fruits in the mouth outlined with a pleasing fruity juiciness. Really nicely fruited, with good depth. Powdery tannins, but finely so. 2 hours later: Full black fruit aromas and flavors. Nice concentration and acidity. Tannins are still grippy and a touch rustic. 24 hours later quite a different wine. Fruit becomes much more complex, savory and cherryish, red and black, and more dried or conserve-like. Texture broadens, becomes more velvety and proportionately, acidity is lessened in the scheme of things. 92

Unnamed, cross border white wine collaboration

Adega Marel & Raúl Moreno-Yague 2021 Granja-Amareleja. *Talha*-fermented blend of Rabo de Ovelha (Sheep's tail), old vine Antão Vaz and Roupeiro, matured four months in 100-year-old, 800-liter, Amontillado (Sherry) Chestnut Barrels. Intriguing fresh floral aromas dressed in a sweet atmospheric lift from sherry barrels. A very interesting wine. Rounded and sweetly fruited, grapey, juicy, and viscous, with fruit sweetness beautifully balanced by acidity. A classy, new wine style with nice length. Given airing it develops fresh celery leaf, flower stem aromas, becoming fuller bodied, but not at all heavy. Lots of fresh, juicy fruits well up after swallowing. 90

El Resplandor Branco Sin Fronteiras Bromco 2021 12.5%. Made with crushed Portuguese white grapes but only uses Roupeiro skins enclosed in a bag that's steeped in the *talha*, like making tea. Quite minerally with a rounded middle and finely tapered finish. 88

Adega Marel Slate n Chalk Sin Fronteiras Tinto 2021. A cross border 'EU' designated wine produced in *talha* that blends Portuguese Moreto and Trincadeira with Spanish Tintilla de Rota (father of Graciano). Opens with toasty, roasted oak aromas from time spent in 500-liter oak barrels. Offers tons of sappy, savory red fruit aromas and flavors. Tintilla has lip smacking high acidity that *talha* rounds out into plush textures. I liked it so much I forgot to score it.

Chapter 21
Herdade dos Outeiros Altos

Sub-region: Borba
Address: Monte da Tapada Nova, C. P. nº 11, Sta Maria, 7100-123 Estremoz, Portugal
Owners/Winemakers: Jorge Cardoso and Fernanda Rodrigues
Phone: +351 966250063
Email: info@herdadedosouteirosaltos.pt
Website: www.herdadedosouteirosaltos.pt
General Information:
Vineyard: 14 hectares
Talha: 28, 150-1200ltr

Outeiros Altos (meaning high hills) is all about masterful grape growing and careful winemaking. Jorge Cardoso and Fernanda Rodrigues, both university-trained agronomists, are true vignerons, focused on growing grapes perfectly suited to their site and making wine that reflects this as transparently as possible. Their commitment to *talha* is a natural extension of this philosophy.

They began searching for the perfect vineyard site in 1999, eventually establishing Herdade dos Outeiros Altos within Serra d'Ossa's mountainous country south of Estremoz.

In 2002 they planted their three vineyards (14 hectares) in a mixture of schist and quartz soils within a bowl-shaped, gentle slope astride the Outeiros Altos hills at 350 meters. After making Alentejo's first certified Organic DOC wines, they eventually moved on to more intensive biodynamic and natural production, with the first Alentejo's natural DOC wine following in 2016.

At 650 meters, the Serra d'Ossa range creates a protective micro-climate that delivers ample rainfall (and occasionally snow), cooler nights and fresh foggy summer mornings that positively impact vines. Wines are effectively blended in the vineyard, with grapes selected from up to six varieties, depending on preferred levels of ripeness and their potential to create the best balance between fruit and structure each season.

In keeping with transparency, wine production is fundamentally natural and chemical-free, relying only on spontaneous fermentation and relatively low, if any, sulfite additions. Wine production, totalling 15,000 bottles, is not exclusively focused on *talha*, with some wine made more conventionally in stainless steel and matured in old, neutral French oak barrels. Both the basic range and the 'sulfite free' wine follow that formula. Their reserve wine is a hybrid, not unlike Jose de Sousa's Major; it is fermented in *talha*, then aged in French oak.

Their pure *talha* wines are certified Vinho de Talha DOC, staying on 'mother' at least until November's St. Martin's Day before bottling. Depending on the season, the red ranges between 1,000 to 4,000 bottles and the white produces around 600 bottles. Outeiros Altos have 28 *talha* ranging from 150 to 1200 liters, all bought - at considerable cost - off the local market. Most were manufactured in São Pedro do Corval (formerly Aldeia do Mato), Campo Maior, Amieira do Tejo (Nisa municipality), Évora or are of undetermined origin. Remarkably, one is dated 1666, one of the oldest in the country.

Mastering how to make wine in each one of these is a slow, methodical process of discovery. But clearly they've made considerable progress so far. Jorge said his white wine 'reminds him of the wines he drank as a young man' suggesting his strategies have been able to reproduce the traditional styles he hoped he could replicate.

One comment Jorge made was quite insightful to unlocking the mystery of *pés* in former times. He noted he was very careful with *pés* application. Not wanting to burn the wax and leech smoky/burned characters into the wine, he

Herdade dos Outeiros Altos

avoids heating an inverted *talha* over an open flame fire, opting instead to apply *pés* more precisely with a blow torch. In all of my conversations so far, no one else had mentioned this. Perhaps his strategy is due to his sensitivity towards maintaining vineyard-derived fruit expression that he works so hard to create most of the year. Outeiros Altos's *talha* wines are relatively transparent and seem a pure reflection of the fruit of their vines.

Very much active custodians of their land, the owners of Outeiros Altos are as much about farming and restoring biodiversity as making wine. Growing olive and quince trees, organically of course, they produce oil and olives from the former and Portuguese *marmalada* from the latter. The place teems with life, abounding in birds, insects and many types of herbs and flowers, as well as bees that produce intensely flavored honey.

This visionary couple are creating a much richer environment than the one they found.

White wine

Outeiros Altos Talha Branco 2020 12.5%. A super clean and fresh blend of Antão Vaz and Arinto filled with lovely floral aromas. Quite a remarkable perfume to this wine: subtle marshmallow vanilla (oak free?) meringue and orange blossom notes. Full bodied, with a rounded texture that leans out into a long, elegantly tapered finish, laced with fine acidity. 92/100

Red wines

Outeiros Altos Talha Tinto 2020 14.5% Vinho de Talha DOC. A traditional local blend of Aragonez, Alfrocheiro and Trincadeira, with just a touch of Alicante Bouchet and Touriga Nacional. I found this surprisingly fresh for such a higher alcohol wine. Full of quite pure black cherry, plum and black fruit characters. These played out flavor-wise at mid-palate with an unexpected juiciness and degree of elegance struck through with fine acidity running throughout a long finish. Quaffable now, but promising even more in future. 96

Outeiros Altos Talha Tinto 2019 15% Vinho de Talha DOC. A traditional local blend of Aragonez, Alfrocheiro and Trincadeira, with Alicante Bouchet and a little more Touriga Nacional this year for added tannic support. From a hotter vintage that created more cooked fruit, raisined characters. Fuller, richer in the mouth than the 2020 with over-ripe, raisiny fruit flavors and considerably grippier tannins. Less successful for my tastes. 88

Outeiros Altos Talha Tinto 2018 14.5% Vinho de Talha DOC. A traditional local blend of (mostly) Trincadeira, Alfrocheiro and Aragonez. Deeply concentrated and broader in the mouth than the 2020. Nice balance of tannins and perfectly ripe fruit. 92

Outeiros Altos Talha 2017 14% Vinho de Talha DOC. Lots of transparent, clearly passionately grown fruit in this wine made from Aragonez, Alfrocheiro and Trincadeira. Although from a very hot year, it doesn't show 'hot' characters. Quite tightly closed up initially. After airing, an ever expanding bouquet is dressed with a mineral, graphite complexity that glosses over a mix of dried, and not so dried, black fruit characters. It's a sexy, adult kind of wine. Seamless, finely textured and highly concentrated in the mouth with a long, long finish. I particularly liked the honest skin tannins, balancing acidity in harmonious support. From a hot year, surprisingly, it honestly illustrates that seasonal influence without being cooked or overblown or spirity. 97

Talha room and sleeping dog at Outeiros Altos

Chapter 22
Quinta da Pigarça & Adega do Canena

Subregion: Vidigueira
Quinta da Pigarça
Address: 7940-000 Cuba, Portugal
GPS: Lon: 7.89871W Lat: 38.17713N
E-mail: geral@quintadapigarca.pt
Phone: +351 284 412 210
Website: http://quintadapigarca.pt
Winemaking team: Joao Canena, his father, brother and co-winemaker Mauro Azoia
Adega do Canena
Address: Travessa Cândido dos Reis 11, 7940-108 Cuba, Portugal
Phone: +351 960 099 077

Joao and Susana Canena

Over the last few years the Canena family's Quinta da Pigarça has stealthily become Alentejo's largest producer of *talha* wine, currently making over 100,000 liters (133,000 bottles) in 150 *talha*. Their oldest *talha* is from 1655, but most are from the classic 1800s era. Ranging in size from 600, 1100, 1300 and 1500 liters, Pigarça also has the largest *talha* on earth - an extraordinary whopper at 8000 liters!

Winemaker Joao Canena completed his first harvest in 1997, readily admitting he didn't initially like wine very much. Now he probably makes more clay-fermented wine than anyone on earth. Like others of his generation, he carries on a deep family tradition following on from his father, who made *talha* wine at Herdade do Rocim's old adega in the 1970s and his grandfather, going way back into the 1930s, making *talha* wine at Casa Field in what is now Cuba's municipal museum.

Previously the quinta's focus was high-volume, conventionally-made wine that had topped out around one million liters. But inspired by *talha* wine's rising star, the family has returned to its roots and is increasingly focused on producing large volumes of high-quality *talha* wine.

Quinta da Pigarça - the silent giant of *talha* wine production

Although trained in modern winemaking techniques, Joao makes it clear that traditional practices passed down through his family were equally important, 'I was born watching and helping my grandfather and father produce *talha* wine and at that time I fell in love with the natural process of turning grapes into wine.' The oral traditions passed down through this generational continuity have proved essential in mastering *talha* technology. Pigarça's *talhas*, for example, are *pés* lined with a mix of pitch and beeswax, applied by the family, when needed, according to their own time-tested recipes that reach back into the 19th century.

Of the 100,000 liters made in *talha*, Quinta da Pigarça bottles about 50,000-60,000 liters and Canena around 15,000. All of their brands are certified Vinhos de Talha DOC, with the rest of the wine sold off in bulk. As per DOC certification, wines are taken off their mother between December and February. From that point wines are either bottled, or moved to cleaned *talha,* or into special clay barrels for further maturation. Pigarça owns a unique collection of these barrique-shaped clay pots inherited from an earlier generation making *talha* wine in the 19th century.

I first saw photos of these clay barrels at Amphora Day 2018. It was a stunning revelation. Beautiful in their own right, these purposefully designed and skillfully executed terracotta containers proved that clay maturation was a local practice in the past. This not only suggests that not all *talha* wine was intended to be drunk up in the first year, but also that winemakers were actively choosing to mature in small-format clay containers instead of larger *talha*. These smaller clay barrels would oxidize the wines faster, resulting in fuller, more polished textures and softer tannins. Of

Pigarça's rare barrique shaped clay pots

course, another highly significant point is that the choice of a barrel shape and size - and purposefully made of clay - suggests an early clear preference for terracotta conditioning over wood.

Pigarça use clay barrels in both *talha* and conventional wine making. Some of their 'modern style' whites and reds are fermented in clay barrels (without *pés*), replacing oak barrel fermentation and maturation practices. Similarly, some of their *talha*-fermented reds are also aged in clay barrels, somewhat akin to Herdade do Rocim's 'clay aged' wine matured in small clay jugs.

The quinta's vineyard holdings total 25 hectares, with vines between four and forty years old. A quarter of this is in whites: Antao vaz, Roupeiro, Arinto, Perrum, Diegalves, Rabo de Ovelha, with the rest in reds: Trincadeira, Aragones, Tinta Grossa, Touriga Nacional, Moreto, Alfrocheiro, Alicante Bouchet.

Supplementary fruit comes from other small vineyards they own near Cuba and Vidigueira, all within 10km of the quinta. Many of these are traditional, mixed variety, field blends, including an impressive two hectares of 80+ year old vines planted on their own roots. They also buy grapes from old upland vines in the Vila Alva region.

Quinta da Pigarça is very much a traditional, self-contained, working farm, not purely focused on just growing grapes and making wine. Historically, their main business has been olive oil supported by other farming activities, including raising black Iberian pigs (manufacturing their own sausage and dry ham), *touro de lide* (Spanish fighting bulls), wild boars and game birds. The quinta also contains agro tourism apartments and has a large restaurant on site, renowned locally for its traditional, home-cooked recipes supplied from the farm.

Recently the family purchased an old adega inside the town of Cuba. This will become the new home of Adega do Canena, also functioning as a traditional urban *taberna* with an additional greatly enlarged restaurant area as well. Plans are afoot to extend and shift Quinta da Pigarça's *talha* production into a newly designed winery.

Joao Canena gravitated back into *talha* wine because of the 'uniqueness of producing a natural wine like the Romans, without [modern] technologies they were able to do [without] 2000 years ago.' His aim is to continue producing 'quality wines, innovative and as natural as possible.'

As large as Pigarça and Canena are now, it's clear they have even bigger plans for the future.

White wines

Canena Vinhas Velhas Branco 2022. Destined to be a Vinho de Talha DOC. A blend of 30-year-old vine Perrun and Diagalves. An ultra-minerally, savory style, with fruit density, good concentration and fine grippy, skin tannins. 90/100

Canena Branco 2020 13.5% Vinho de Talha DOC. A blended mixture of old vine Antão Vaz, Roupeiro and Arinto. Offers up spicy, fresh herb and vegetal aromas. Fruit has a ripe sweetness, but also savory edge at same time, indescribably so. Full bodied, dense and concentrated in the mouth with a fine viscosity and degree of unctuous oiliness. Good length and balanced acidity. 89

Canena Roupeiro 2020 Vinho de Talha DOC. A very fine, tight wine with good length. Smelling of seashells, minerals and delicately fresh blossoms. Very pure, with laser sharp focus and superb acid balance. Good length. 92

Canena Branco 2020 Vinho de Talha DOC 13.5%. A blended mixture of old vine Antão Vaz, Roupeiro and Arinto. Offers up spicy, fresh herb and vegetal aromas. Fruit has a ripe sweetness, but also savory edge at same time, indescribably so. Full bodied, dense and concentrated in the mouth with a fine viscosity and degree of unctuous oiliness. Good length and balanced acidity. 89

Quinta da Pigarça Branco 2018 Vinho de Talha DOC 12.5%. A blended mixture of old vine Antão Vaz, Roupeiro and Arinto. Quite yellow in color, but not advanced or oxidized. Mineral with touch of spice, fine slick, well integrated texture, finish, seamless linear style with balancing acidity. 93

Red wines

Canena Tinto 2022. Destined to be a Vinho de Talha DOC wine tasted fresh from *talha*. A blend of 30-year-old vine Aragonez, Trincadeira, Tinta Grossa and Moreto. aromas, aromas, A slick and creamy smooth wine with continuous textures and long-grained, fine tannins. Aromas offered up a complex mix of florals, mushroom and mulberry characters. A terrific wine. 93

Canena Tinto 2020 Vinho de Talha DOC. A very clean savory style with a mix of slight roasted, dried red and black fruit characters. Textures are creamy smooth with finely balanced acids and tannins. 89

Quinta da Pigarça Tinto 2018 14.5% Vinho de Talha DOC. A blend of old vine Aragonez, Trincadeira, Tinta Grossa and Moreto. Opens with a savory mix of dried red and black fruit aromas with mineral gloss. Bouquet is nicely married into itself. Full bodied with cherryish acidity cutting though. Quite a clean feeling to the wine. Well balanced. After airing, first time I smelled pine needles and tastes of a burning beeswax candle, possible hints of fresh *pés*? (tasted 10/21) 90

Quinta da Pigarça Tinto 2018 14.5% Vinho de Talha DOC. A blend of old vine Aragonez, Trincadeira, Tinta Grossa and Moreto.   This has dried stem, dried herbal high notes, over a baseline of minerality and dried red fruit characters. Nicely fruited up front in the mouth, showing a slight smokiness/roasted edge to fruit flavors (possible *pés* derived cooked beeswax notes?). Continuous and concentrated textures in the mouth, structured with firm acidity and fine, but firm, tannins. Good length of flavor. A subtle persistence wine, not overwhelmingly fruity, but one that grows on you halfway down the bottle. (Retasted 12.21) 90

Canena Tinto 2017 15% Vinho de Talha DOC. A blend of old vine Aragonez, Trincadeira, Tinta Grossa and Moreto. Offers a mixture of dried fruits and blackberry-strawberry jam aromas and flavors. A very full-bodied wine, bolstered by a strong streak of alcoholic glycerin running throughout. An ultra-ripe style with just enough acidity to balance. I found it overly hot and heavy back when I first tried it in Alentejo's August's heat, but now in December, as a storm rages outside the old Cornish fisherman's cottage I'm inhabiting, it turned out to be a perfect winter wine to accompany the roasted lamb I'm eating at the moment. Tasted 7.12.21 3rd retasting 28.3.22. The wine was served in a very different context, dining (beef bourguignon) with friends who were winemakers. This time the wine was more linear, less overtly alcoholic and well liked for its smooth texture and balancing acidity. 89

Palhete

Canena Palhete 2022. This mix of co-fermented white and red grapes lean toward 'eye of swan' blush color. Fruits are of mix of peach and strawberryish notes carried through a fullish body, ending with a fine, tight, mineral finish and firm acidity. Good length. 89

Other stylistic experiments

Experimental Sparkling wine made in *talha*. No doubt a first for *talha*, but there is precedent with one Champagne producer using amphora as part of its processing. This displayed very fine bubbles and a degree of finesse, suggesting excellent potential. The quality of bubbles and mousse was especially good.

Chapter 23
Casa Relvas

Sub-region: Evora
Address: Herdade São Miguel de Machede, Évora 7005-752 Portugal
Owner/Winemakers: Relvas family
Email: info@casarelvas.pt.
Phone: +351 266 988 034
Website: https: //www.casarelvasandfriends.pt/en/

With deep roots in Africa and coming from outside the wine industry, Alexandre Relvas established Casa Relvas in 1997. Over the years it has grown into a large, modern, technologically-driven wine company producing over seven million bottles of wine, sold under a dozen brands to 35 countries. Production is not exclusively devoted to wine, with Merino sheep, cork and olive trees in the mix as well. This is very much a modern, super-efficient agribusiness focused on what Alentejo does best.

Over time, company management has been handed on from Alexandre (Sr.) to his two sons, Alexandre and António. These likeable, enthusiastic, 30-somethings have shifted Relvas's philosophical focus towards high-quality, terroir-focused production and sustainable organic practices.

Alexandre Relvas in his *talha* room

During the last few years they've turned their attention to *talha*-made wine, aiming for something authentic and traditional that speaks of Alentejo. 'Something,' Alexandre says, 'people can enjoy and share around a table.' Quite unexpectedly, their Art.Terra Amphora red has turned out to be one of the biggest selling wines in their shop.

The company draws grapes primarily from two large estates, Herdade Sao de Miguel (35 ha) and Herdade da Pimenta (60 ha), located on the plains halfway between Evora and Redondo. More recently they've acquired 155 hectares of warmer climate vineyards near Vidigueira to the south, and 25 near Evora. Vines are around 20-30 years old and 20 hectares are certified organic. All this allows Casa Relvas to draw differing fruit characters from a range of elevations and sub-climates.

A family of *talha*

Casa Relvas make their Art.Terra range in 14 *talha* in sizes ranging from 200 to 1500 liters. All are coated in *pés*. But, interestingly, they use two versions of the traditional mix of resin, beeswax and a secret herbal mixture. One is darker and the other a lighter, golden color. The latter they reckon creates a more elegant wine.

They follow the traditional practice of placing stems in the bottom of *talha* to provide natural filtering and hold the wine on 'mother' for three months with bottling in January. Most of their grapes are broken up before (wild yeast) fermentation, but sometimes they add whole bunches to amplify aromatics. Alexandre thinks *talhas* produce 'lots of oxidation early during fermentation, keeping the wine stable and fresh.' The white is pure Arinto (unusual), transferred from *talha* into stainless steel and bottled quickly. The red is a co-fermentation of Trincadeira, Aragonez and Moreto bottled in January.

Alexandre offered some insightful observations on how modern consumers experience *talha* wines. Referring back to how the red amphora wine was a big seller at the winery shop, 'whites are more difficult for customers to understand or appreciate.' Talha whites simply aren't your average 'everyday wine' for modern taste. He was alluding to the skin tannins which naturally inhabit all reds but most people don't expect in whites today. Their appreciation will require a generational shift in taste, skipping back to what was normal a couple of generations ago.

A confusing aspect here is that they label their Art.Terra range as 'Amphora' although they tick all the right traditional boxes for Vinho de Talha DOC status. The contradiction is that although all the grapes they make into *talha* wine are grown in DOC regions, their winery is not located in any 'official' DOC region, so their wine can't be officially certified as Vinho de Talha DOC wine. Hence, they must call it a 'regional amphora' wine instead.

From a standpoint outside of Alentejo this all seems a little crazy, but 'them's the rules' and up to locals to sort out for themselves. While 'amphora' designation actually allows Casa Relvas a lot more freedom to make their *talha* wine however they want, they still prefer to follow the traditional guidelines anyway.

It all begs a question. While Casa Relvas may technically be outside the DOC now, going back 25 or 50 or 100 or 2000 years, it would have been considered *talha* wine like anywhere else in Alentejo.

White wines

Art.Terra Amphora Branco 2018 11.5%. 100% Arinto after one year of age. Bright golden color. Opens with flower stem aromas. Gently rounded on entry with nice fruit density laced with green almond undertones and supported by fine lemony acidity. Shows Arinto's floral and linear characters well. Tasted August 2021. 88/100

Art.Terra Amphora 2018 11.5%. 100% Arinto, fresh from *talha* and still on skins. Offers lifted florals with hints of (*pés* influenced) beeswax, honey and lemon. Has a very fine, slick, waxy texture and fine acidity. Pears and lemon flavors well up on finish. Nice length. Tasted fresh St. Martin's Day 2018. 90

Art.Terra 2017 Arinto. Tasted fresh from *talha*. Shows a pronounced, newly applied *pés* influence. Pleasing mix of honey wax and hints of pine resin. But long on orange characters too. Full bodied on entry, but leans out towards finish. Marmalade-like quince & orange fruits throughout with flavors of pine and wax and marmalade welling up on finish. Tasted St. Martin's Day 2018. 88

Art.Terra Amphora 2017. Tasted January 2019. Dark yellow with quince mineral aromas and flavors. Very slick continuous texture, with this being the wine's strong point. 87

Art.Terra Amphora 2017. 100% Arinto tasted a year later, November 2019. Spiky, spicy aromas, nice balanced texture, still fresh, although acidity is a bit grippy. 87

Red wines

Art.Terra Amphora Tinto 2020 13.5%. A quaffable summer wine made from a co-fermented blend of Trincadeira, Aragonez and Moreto bottled in January. Fresh, lively dried herb, red fruit and mineral stoneware characters. Creamy smooth, with refreshingly pure fruits and great length of flavor. Tasted August 2021. 94

Art.Terra Amphora Tinto 2018. A co-fermented blend of Trincadeira, Aragonez and Moreto, 1/3 each. Lots of personality in this wine. Brightly lit mix of red and black fruits and savory meaty aromas. This develops an additional, interesting mineral and coffee nuances. Soft and full bodied texture initially in the mouth. Then juicy skin tannins emerge with wine changing into something much more linear. Tasted St. Martin's Day 2018. 90

Art.Terra Tinto 2017. A 1/3 each blend of Trincadeira, Aragonez and Moreto kept in *talha* with skins for four months. Pressed, then transferred to 100-liter *talha* for 3 months ageing. Spicy, honeyed and packed with red fruit and black cherry flavors. Edgy in the mouth with firm tannins, balanced by fruits and fine acidity. Lots of personality and good flavor length. Tasted St. Martin's Day 2018. Second tasting January 2019. A mix of brambly blackfruit aromas and menthol notes. Even more brambly blackfruits in the mouth, kept in check by very fine, powdery mid-palate tannins that carry through the finish. Tons of expansive fruit in this wine, nicely underpinned with balancing structure. 91

Art.Terra Amphora Tinto 2016 13.5% A crowd pleasing blend of Trincadeira, Aragonez and Moreto that was one of their biggest sellers at their winery shop. Tons of roasted black fruit characters, with a continuous texture, firm acidity and fine firm tannins. A lot of juicy, black cherry fruit wells up after swallowing. Tasted at Terracotta Wines 9.2018. 90

Art.Terra Amphora Tinto 2016 13.5%. A wine of great purity and honesty, showing its blend of Trincadeira, Aragonez and Moreto well. Packed with fresh ultra pure red and black fruit aromatics and flavors. Tannins are honest and out there, although not overly aggressive. Nice wine. Tasted St. Martin's Day 11.2018. 89

Art.Terra Amphora Tinto 2015 13.5%. Fruit from Herdade Sao Miguel. Spirity, gamey, red fruit aromas and flavors, very fine, firm tannins with tons of red fruit on finish. A well-fruited wine with balanced acidity, good length and a degree of elegance. Great example of new wave *talha* wine. 90

Chapter 24
Herdade do Rocim

Subregion: Vidigueira
Address: Estrada Nacional 387 Apartado 64 7940-909 Cuba Alentejo Portugal
GPS: 38º 11' 50.0"N 7º 51'18.6"W
Team: Pedro Ribeiro, Catarina Vieira, Pedro Pegas
Phone: +351 284 415 180
Email: herdadedorocim@herdadedorocim.com
Website: https://rocim.pt/en/

Passionate supporters of the *talha* revival, Herdade do Rocim's dynamic husband-and-wife team, Pedro Ribeiro and Catarina Vieira, have accomplished a great deal of very good things over the last decade. Exporting various forms of *talha* wine to thirty countries on five continents, they have helped place both Alentejo and *talha* wine on the global wine map. Along the way their smartly cast brands have introduced thousands of younger drinkers to fresh, clean, consumer-friendly wine, made (implausibly to some) in ancient earthen-ware pots.

Catarina Vieira, Pedro Ribeiro and Pedro Pegas of Rocim

Equally important, they've drawn wine tourists into the heart of *talha* country through their annual Amphora Wine Day, showcasing clay-made wine from around the world sitting alongside St. Martin's Day's freshly minted, local *talha* wines.

Beyond producing Vinho de Talha DOC wine, Rocim have expanded the stylistic horizon of what *talha* technology is capable of creating, through brands focused on clay-aged, natural and amphora designations, topping all this off with a premium's premium 1000 euro *talha* wine, called Jupiter. After selling out in a few days, this became the most expensive clay-made wine anywhere on earth, proving clay can compete with the world's top conventionally made wines.

The forty-something couple are university trained in wine and manage Rocim together as equal partners. Ribeiro is focused more on winemaking and promotional globetrotting, with Vieira overseeing the vineyard and keeping the winery's doors open.

The original Herdade do Rocim 120-hectare estate was purchased in 2000 by Terralis Lda, a Portuguese agricultural machinery company intent on regenerating the vineyards and building a state-of-the-art winery. This included a traditional twenty-hectare, field-blended, mixed-variety vineyard, Vinha do Olho de Mocho. Seventy-five years old now, this has proved an important core of production.

Originally conceived to produce modern technologically driven wines, the vineyards have seen a steady planting program over the last twenty years expanding up to seventy-four hectares, with another thirty hectares rented elsewhere. The bulk of this is in local Portuguese grapes (Aragonez, Trincadeira, Moreto, Tinta Grossa and whites Antão Vaz, Rabo de Ovelha, Perrum, Roupeiro and Mantuedo), but also includes French varieties: Syrah, Cabernet Sauvignon, Tannat and Petit Verdot. Northern Portuguese white grapes have also been added over time: Arinto, Verdelho, Viosinho and Alvarinho. All of this provides lots of material to play around with either as modern, conventional single varietal and multi-blended wines or newly evolved traditional styles.

In 2015 they added Vinha de Micaela, a tiny (.36 hectare) 80+ year-old vineyard from a neighbor, planted in Moreto, Tinta Grossa, Trincadeira, Alicante Bouschet and various other grapes. They've gained organic certification for some vineyards and most recently the whole property achieved Alentejo's official sustainability certification.

So good grape growing no doubt plays a huge role in the quality and qualities of Rocim's wines.

Vieira studied in Portugal and Italy, learning both modern and traditional vine management, 'always trying to understand different kinds of viticulture, different philosophies, looking for more than the usual. There are no new concepts without knowing so well the old ones.' For her, 'the beauty is to combine the new concepts with the old ones, improving of course quality and always respecting the terroir.'

Whereas new vineyards were planted in respect to how they fit into Rocim's terroir, the older vines in Vinha do Olho de Mocho or Vinha de Micaela were maintained in traditional growing practices. Vieira says, 'exactly the same way, with minimal intervention.' Noticing differences between the old vines versus the newly planted ones she observed, 'the old vines gave us more complexity, deepness, an excellent balance and volume.'

Vieira believes that the grapes common around Cuba, Vidigueira, Frades and Vila Alva are 'very well adapted to *talha* vinification. The *talhas* promote more freshness, softer tanins, ….We pick the grapes earlier than is usual in the region, we believe the acidity is very important in this kind of wine.'

A new winery was built in 2007 in front of the original Herdade do Rocim's ancient farmhouse and adega. Designed by an award-winning Portuguese architect, Carlos Vitorino, it was constructed along energy-efficient, ecologically friendly lines. Stealthily positioned, half-submerged into the terrain, it is graced by superb panoramic views of the surrounding vineyard slopes. Its sunken cellar and rammed mud wall surround a glassed-in central courtyard with an internal amphitheater - as stunning as it is sustainable.

Packed full of modern winemaking's state-of-the-art technological toys: stainless steel everywhere, French oak barrels, large conical concrete tanks, etc. it also has a full complement of traditional Portuguese wine tools: marble lagars for foot treading, *talha* and small 140-liter clay maturation jugs. The 'new' old Portuguese technology is now a tried-and-tested natural progression beyond conventional 'modernist' winemaking. Producing about a million bottles of wine now, over 40,000 are made in clay.

And then, around 2010, Rocim began shifting its attention towards Alentejo's traditional winemaking technologies, grape blends and vineyard practices. The young team started seriously thinking about *talha* wine.

Historically the old original Herdade do Rocim's *talha* wines were highly respected throughout the region, suggesting the marriage between vineyards and its original adega were capable of something special. And so when

Rocim's eco-friendly modern winery

Rocim returned to *talha* winemaking in 2012, production was restored to the old adega behind the modern complex. Strengthening the re-connection, they turned to Rocim's viticulturist, Pedro Pegas, to make the first wines. Originally from Vidigueira, he had learned the art of *talha* from his 80-year-old father, and has been central to the winemaking team since.

Rocim's first modern *talha* wines came from the quinta's original, field-blend vineyard. This had been replanted from an earlier vineyard in the same local mixture, connecting it back to the early 20th century and possibly even further back: reds, Aragonez 50%, Trincadeira 30%, Moreto 10%, Tinta Grossa 10% and whites, Antão Vaz 40%, Perrum 20%, Rabo de Ovelha 20% and Mantuedo 20%. Fittingly, this was Rocim's oldest, purest terroir.

Since then, both red and white 'amphora' wines have been traditionally made following Vinho de Talha DOC guidelines: unsulphured, made with whole clusters, all stems and skins left to ferment and macerate for two months until St. Martin's Day, then certified and bottled.

Herdade do Rocim's winery - scene of Amphora Day celebrations

I have followed these wines for several years now and they are consistently among my favorite *talha* wine: fresh, purely fruited, with a degree of elegance and remarkably modern in style. What every human, by right, deserves to drink every day of the year. Which when it comes right down to it, is the essence of *talha* wine.

This runs true for most of Herdade do Rocim's other *talha* styles (clay-aged, natural, amphora and Jupiter), which are generally fresher, cleaner and quite appealing to modern tastes.

Part of this is accomplished via approaching *talha* as a technology rather than a strict adherence to a concept of tradition. Aiming for a purer interaction between wine and clay, they don't line with *pés*, to avoid any added flavors and aromas. Similarly, they don't protect the wine's surface from oxidation with an added layer of flavor-filled olive oil, opting for a floating silicon disk instead.

I recall Ribeiro once mentioning, with an ironic wink, that 'traditionally there was more variability in how tannins were managed in the past, by adjusting skin contact.' Alas, because current DOC regulations require photographic evidence of grapes contained in the *talha* after St. Martin's Day, this is no longer possible. Countering that requires diligence and close attention to how well the wines are evolving.

Beyond their *talha* DOC wines, Rocim make 'Fresh from Amphora' natural wines, with less intervention, no added chemicals and at lower alcohol of 11.5%. It is uncertified DOC because they remove it from skins immediately after fermentation to preserve fresher fruit characters. They come in larger 1-liter bottles and are what they suggest: fresh, fruity and highly quaffable.

In many ways Rocim have grabbed the baton following in Jose de Sousa's footsteps, playing around with *talha* and *lagar* fermentation and substituting clay maturation for oak barrel conditioning.

The first of these projects was their 'aged in clay' wines. These were foot-trodden in large stone *lagars*, then left in them to fully ferment, and thereafter moved into small 140-liter jug-shaped pots to mature. These replaced conventional oak barrel ageing with the advantage of not infusing the wines with oak flavors, aromas and bitter tannins. Beyond their relative neutrality, they burnish the wine's textures with micro-oxidation at about twice the rate of wooden barrels. This results in purer fruit characters and softer textures.

Rocim's 'aged in clay' wines are aged in 140 liter jug-shaped pots

The wines use northern Portuguese grapes: Verdelho, Viosinho and Alvarinho. Whereas the reds were originally built around Alicante Bouchet and Trincadeira, with French grapes Petit Verdot and Tannat. They eventually traded in the French for a Portuguese grape with a French name, Touriga Franca. Quinta da Pigarca use barrel-shaped clay vessels to produce a similar style of wine.

Pedro Ribeira also produces *talha*-made wine outside the Rocim range. His own Bojador brand is Vinho de Talha DOC but produced from rented vineyards in Vidigueira. Blends change according to the seasonal variation with whites kept on skins for five months and reds an additional one or two. And from further afield he makes Santiago na Anfora do Rocim, a very polished Alvarinho from its homeland, Moncao e Melgaco, in the Vinho Verde region.

But the most spectacularly successful of these experimental projects is Jupiter. Originally destined for Rocim's baseline Vinho de Talha DOC range, when Ribeiro first tasted this wine he realized it was the best wine he'd ever made. Instead of bottling, he moved the wine to a cleaned *talha* to age longer. Checking it religiously for any decline in quality, instead the wine only got better. After an unheard of four years in *talha* it was finally bottled. Priced at 1000eu Jupiter sold out within days. Not only Portugal's most expensive wine ever, but the most expensive clay-pot-made wine from anywhere, ever. Jupiter managed to knock the ball out of the stadium in terms of what clay-made wine could accomplish.

Sometimes it takes someone from the outside to see what is most special about a place. Ribeiro and Vieira, both from other parts of Portugal, have done just that, embracing the essence of what makes this part of Alentejo unique in the world. Their love for what they have found has inspired them to take that message out into the greater world for the betterment of *talha* culture and their community.

The Wines

Herdade do Rocim Amphora (Vinho de Talha DOC)

10,000 bottles of Red and 10,000 bottles of White.

I love both Herdade do Rocim Amphora Vinho de Talha DOC whites and reds to pieces. Drink these babies at their best - under a year old - and they are definitely most fun when poured, on Amphora Day, straight out of the *talha* that made them.

White Wines

Herdade do Rocim Amphora Branco 2022 ??%. Tasted straight from *talha* on St Martins weekend at Amphora Wine Day 2022 and destined to become Vinho de Talha DOC. This year's season produced intense grapefruit and tropical aromas and flavors. It could easily have passed for young Sauvignon Blanc. A succulent, lip-smacking wine if ever there was one. 90/100

Herdade do Rocim Amphora Branco 2021 12% Vinho de Talha DOC. This white has lovely floral and citrus characters. Creamy smooth in the mouth, this cut through with tart, clean, edgy, acidity. Simple, direct and so pure. 89

Herdade do Rocim Amphora Branco 2020 13% Vinho de Talha DOC. From a warmer vintage so a little rounder, slicker and fuller bodied than previous year, but still retains the lines delicate florals and lazer sharp, lemony-saline acidity. A great wine for its type.(Tasted 7 & 9.2022) 89-90

Herdade do Rocim Amphora Branco 2018 13% Vinho de Talha DOC. Bright yellow. Neutralish, slightly grapey aromas. A well-rounded and fullish-bodied wine tasting of fresh, juicy white table grapes (Thomson seedless). Nicely balancing acidity. In the middle of drinking this I thought it was reminiscent of good quality 'unwooded' chardonnay with the full-bodied texture that Chardonnay drinkers like, plus the minerality that Burgundy drinkers like, along with a good whack of balancing acidity. (Tasted 2019) 89

Herdade do Rocim Amphora Branco 2018 13% Vinho de Talha DOC. Tasted at a year and a half of age, it's still quite a fresh wine, smelling of flower stems and aloe vera. Full-bodied and dense, but with sharp acidity cutting through. Quite minerally and juicy white grape characters throughout. (Tasted 5.20) 89

Herdade do Rocim Amphora Branco 2017 12% Vinho de Talha DOC. Deep yellow colored. A blend of Antao Vaz 40% Perrum 20% Rabo de Ovelha 20% Mateudo 20%. Texturally, this reminds me of a minerally driven mature Meursault from a ripe year. Very ripe flavors this vintage with subtle orange peel, mango, dried apricot characters. These are more nuanced than overt. Nice fresh orange/mandarin citrus acidity up front and throughout. Tapered in mouth, sneaking up, growing, then tapering off. Retasted an hour later, it develops a lovely juiciness throughout. Quite fresh acidity. Subtle, complex, well integrated mix of flavors and aromas. It's so well integrated that there are no dominant aromas or flavors, more a melange. 89-90

Herdade do Rocim Amphora Branco 2015 12% Vinho de Talha DOC. This lovely, low alcohol (12%) blend of 40% Antão Vaz, Rabo de Ovelha, Perrum, Roupeiro and Mantuedo is stylishly modern, indeed surprisingly so. Offering up a heady mix of earthy, meaty, saline and mineral aromas. Quite a lifted nose derived from grape intensity as clearly not alcohol-driven. Follows with a fine texture with a nice juicy acidity and melt-away finish.. Tasted 7.2016 90

Red Wines

Herdade do Rocim Amphora Tinto 2022 ?%. Tasted straight from *talha* on St Martins weekend at Amphora Wine Day 2022 and destined to become Vinho de Talha DOC. Brimming with fresh raspberry-red fruit characters, carried through a plummy, plush texture, delivering great flavor length. A happy little tail-wagger of a wine aiming to please. 90

Herdade do Rocim Amphora Tinto 2021 12% Vinho de Talha DOC. This red is full of fresh cherry and redberry aromas. And then fine, slick and cherryish in the mouth. Love it, so simple, direct and so pure. Remarkable flavor length. I can drink this till the cows come home. At its best under a year old. Tasted 8.2021 90

Herdade do Rocim Amphora Tinto 2020 13% Vinho de Talha DOC. From a warmer vintage and deeper, and more concentrated for it. Lots of crushed berry aromas and flavors with celery leaf high tones. tannins are chunkier and more forceful this year. Quite concentrated and long finishing. 91

Herdade do Rocim Amphora Tinto 2017 12% Vinho de Talha DOC. Moreto 50% Tinta Grossa 30% Trincadeira 15% Aragonez 5%. Broadly aromatic with savory, leathery, slightly herbal red fruit aromas. Light and delicately fruity in the mouth. Fine acidity and fine, firm skin tannins. Two hours later, it maintains initial savory aromatics and purer fruit flavors, becoming more intensively concentrated without gaining girth. Has a deceptively long finish considering the lightness of fruit. Not a huge wine, but well formed and true to type. Tasted 7.2018 90

Herdade do Rocim Amphora Tinto 2015 13.5? Vinho de Talha DOC. This wine was pitch perfect for me, finding the right balance of elegance and finesse and lightness and freshness, something I never expected a terracotta-made wine could produce so readily. Lovely red fruit aromas and flavors carried through a fine balance of natural acidity and fine skin tannins. tasted 2016 17/20 90

Herdade do Rocim *Fresh From Amphora* Nat' Cool

5100 red and 3800 white.

White Wines

Herdade do Rocim *Fresh From Amphora* Nat' Cool Branco 2021 11% . Highly gluggable once again. Very floral this vintage; with a great mix of blossom, flower stems and citrus notes. Full and fleshy in the mouth, cut through with crisp, tightly focused acidity. Refreshingly persistent too. 90

Herdade do Rocim *Fresh From Amphora* Nat' Cool Branco 2020 11%. What I like about this is that it's served up in a 1-liter bottle, big enough to share around with lots of friends. Which kinda sets the stage. Fruit has spicy spearmint high toned aromatics. Rounded and full bodied, viscous texture with lemonade like tartness. A bright cheerful wine, probably like they shared around in Roman times. It's only 11% so you can enjoy lots more - a perfect summer wine. 88

Red Wines

Herdade do Rocim *Fresh From Amphora* **Nat' Cool Tinto 2021** 12%. A brightly lit blend that's been naturally fermented and kept on skin for three months. Packed with cherry characters, silky smooth and laser-focused. Another terrific wine to share around a table with friends. 90

Herdade do Rocim *Fresh From Amphora* **Nat' Cool Tinto 2020** 12%. A blend of Moreto 40%, Tinta Grossa 30%, Trincadeira 30%, naturally fermented and kept on skin for three months. Shows a lovely light, transparent red color, lovely red fruit and red cherry aromas and flavors. An easygoing wine for dinner every night or slightly chilled for outdoor summer get-togethers. Soft, cheerful and highly quaffable. It's also deceptively longer finishing than one would expect from its welcoming personality. 88

Rocim Fresh from Amphora Tinto Nat' Cool 2018. This is a delicious wine full stop. I love wines I can see through and even more, ones I can read through. If I was looking to design an enticing Pinot Noir from another grape, this would be it. Lovely red fruit aromas with a herbal background. Soft and succulent up front, velvety texture, finely viscous finish with just enough acidity to balance plenty of fresh red fruits (cherries/raspberries) to a respectably persistent finish. 88 points for its humble nature, 94 for its pure pleasure.

Bojador Vinho de Talha DOC

3000 bottles of white and 6000 of red

White Wines

'Bojador' Branco 2021 11.5% Vinho De Talha DOC. *Talha*-produced and certified white blend of traditional grapes: 40% Perrum, 30% Roupeiro, 20% Rabo de Ovelha and 10% Mantuedo. Replete with fresh green stem florals, then shifting gears in the mouth to tart lemony fruit up front, streaming through a finely viscous texture, ending on a tart, lemony note of acidity. 91

Bojador' Branco 2020 12% Vinho De Talha DOC. *Talha*-produced and certified white blend of traditional grapes. Lovely floral fresh flower stem, spearmint and quince aromas. Citrus quince tartness, with fine viscosity and juicy citrus tartness welling up on finish. Very good length of flavor. 91

'Bojador' Branco 2016 12% Vinho De Talha DOC. A blend of Perrum 40%, Roupeiro 30%, Rabo de Ovelha 20%, and Mantuedo 10% from a 90 year old field blends. *Talha*-produced and certified. Complex stone fruit like aromas. In the mouth it offers dense fruit concentration and multi-layered textures, spun forward by a fine racy acidity. Tasted 2018 94.......Tasted at five years of age the wine is very amber, with orange peel aromas, full bodied and generous in the mouth, with cidery, cooked peach/quince marmalada flavors and good length. I expected this wine to be well over the hill from its color but was pleasantly surprised. Radically different from its younger sister above. Holding its own, but near its end of life I suspect. Tasted 8.21 87

Red Wines

'Bojador' Tinto 2021 12% Vinho De Talha DOC. *Talha*-fermented Trincadeira 40%, Moreto 30% Tinta Grossa 30% and certified DOC. Shares a lovely transparent, light red, Burgundian color. Lots of spicy, cinnamon and clove notes floating atop red fruit aromas, Silky smooth texture sliced through with rapier-like, fine-grained tannins. A serious, elegant style, tightly knit and minerally, with great length of flavor. This has a long life ahead; hope I can taste it again when it has grown a few whiskers. 97

'Bojador' Tinto 2020 12% Vinho De Talha DOC. *Talha* fermented Trincadeira 40%, Moreto 30% Tinta Grossa 30% and certified DOC. Opens with lovely floral red fruit aromas and tight tart cherryish flavors. And then carries on with a long, long, tartly fruited finish. Great wine this. Flavors lasting after swallowing for well over a minute. Drinking well now but will get better with further ageing. It is an unexpected style from a relatively hot climate that somehow produces a cooler climate, Burgundian/Rioja profile where more normally the region produces more massive and powerful red wines. Impressive styling. The Bojador Tinto is a work of genius. Tasted 12.21 97

'Bojador' Tinto 2016 12.5% Vinho De Talha DOC. *Talha*-fermented Trincadeira 40%, Moreto 30% Tinta Grossa 30%. After DOC certification it was aged another nine months in *talha*. Quite a complex wine with mineral-driven red and black fruit aromas. Full of juicy fruit flavors and beautifully balanced acidity, expansiveness mid-palate and great length. Tasted 2018 96

Herdade do Rocim Clay-Aged

3500 bottles of red and 2000 bottles of white

White Wines

Herdade do Rocim Clay Aged Branco 2020 ?%. A white blend of northern Portuguese Verdelho, Viosinho and Alvarinho grapes, gently foot trodden in open top stone *lagar* troughs and fermented with wild yeast. After, aged in 140-liter clay pots for 9 months. Intriguing aromatic mix of blossoms, flat leaf parsley and quince fruit. This becoming increasingly pronounced with airing. A highly textured wine, visceral, with a streak of tart citrusy acidity for balance. Superb seafood wine. Tasted 2021 91

Herdade do Rocim Clay Aged Branco 2017 13%. This blend of Verdelho, Viosinho and Alvarinho grapes is foot-trodden and fermented *lagar* then aged in 140-liter clay pots for 9 months. Although deep yellow/amber colors, it is not an orange wine at all. Full-bodied with creamy textures laced with stone fruit, peach pit flavors and lowish acidity. A wine for drinking now, with a gentle finish with just enough acidity to cleanse the palate. Somewhat reminiscent of barrel-fermented Chardonnay without the toasted vanilla-oak characters and bitter-oak tannins. For me, not as potentially long-lived as the clay-aged red, but drinking beautifully now. Tasted 1.20 88

Red Wines

Herdade do Rocim Clay Aged Tinto 2019 14%. A blend of Alicante Bouchet, Trincadeira and Touriga Franca that has been foot-trodden and fermented in open top *lagars*. After maturing in 140-liter clay jugs for 14 months. I've tasted this wine a couple of times now and been impressed both times. Initially offers up a mix of dried blackberry, brambly loganberry and red fruit aromas, with firm acidity and tannins. An hour of breathing develops florals with red cherry characters becoming more dominant. More air brings tart morello cherry notes, both dried and fresh. The texture develops a slick viscosity and a degree of linearity and nice flavor length. 24 hours later, black fruit aromas emerge with prunes, fig and date notes. Texture develops a seamless, polished glossy feel with soft tannins and balanced acidity. Drinking quite nicely at the moment. As usual, an interesting, unique style. Tasted 4 & 8.22 93

Herdade do Rocim Clay Aged Tinto 2018 14%. This marks a shift from previous mix of French and Portuguese grapes to just Portuguese: Alicante Bouchet Trincadeira and Touriga Franca. Foot-trodden in open-top lagars with wild yeast ferment, then aged in 140-liter clay pots for 16 months. A complex aromatic mix of red and black fruits on the riper side of the spectrum. Rounded, fullish bodied and soft in the mouth, with respectable fruit concentration. Quite a smooth, polished tannic profile with just enough supporting acidity to lengthen flavor. A thoughtfully conceived blend of these three grapes. The clay maturation blasts all sharp edges off a wine and marries it together quicker, making it very much a wine for drinking soon after bottling. 91

Herdade do Rocim Clay Aged Tinto 2017 14.5%. Naturally fermented and foot trodden in lagars, then matured in 140 liter clay jugs for 16 months. A blend of Portuguese Alicante Bouchet and Trincadeira and French Petit Verdot and Tannat grapes. Florally blackberry/currant fruit aromas and flavors. Plenty of fruit flavors with Tannat's dusty, middle of the mouth, tannins poking through. Nice juicy fruits on finish. Needs more time to develop and soften. Tasted 2018. 89

Herdade do Rocim Clay Aged Tinto 2016 14.5%. Foot Trodden Alicante Bouchet, Petit Verdot, Trincadeira and Tannat grapes fermented in open top lagars grown in vineyards between Cuba and Vidigueira. Aged in small clay 140-liter clay pots for 16 months. Shows spicy high-toned red fruit and coconut (but no oak!?! so part of fruit characters) aromas with a big whiff of spirits. Firm tannins from a blend of relatively firm-tannined grapes. Back-palate concentration and good residual length in linear style of wine. Very young and tight and underdeveloped. Needs a lot of time. Twist here is clay ageing, not fermentation influence. Two hours later, loses coconut, gaining more of Petit Verdot and Trincadeira's florals. Tons of tartly outlined dark fruits, firm, fine, skin tannins all lining up for further development. Complex, interesting, multilayered wine with clay creating an earthy/mineral framework. Quite a long finish. Tasted 7.2018. 93

Herdade do Rocim's Rising Star

800 bottles

Herdade do Rocim's Jupiter 2015. See Jupiter Lift Off chapter for full details of the amazing story behind this wine. On all counts this is a wonderfully complete wine, made from an old field-blend vineyard that has offered up a rich mix of red and black fruit aromas and flavors, harmoniously bleeding into one another, further enriched by a graphite mineral gloss. Highly polished and as slick as it is smooth, all that underpinned with a complex layering of tannins. Pure, plush, concentrated, explosive, mouthfillingly complex… it all leads onward towards a long, perfectly tapered, decrescendo that fittingly plays out with more than ample residual flavors. A pitch perfect wine. 100/100

Non Alentejo *talha*-made Santiago na Anfora do Rocim

2000 bottles

Herdade do Rocim Santiago na Anfora do Rocim 2020 12%. Produced in Vinho Verde's subregion, Moncao e Melgaco. Alvarinho's typically floral and lemony aromas. Full and mouth-filling with great citrus-lemony tartness to it. This slides its way through a long, slick and slippery finish. This Alvarinho is all about texture with a finely viscous, glycerine-like feel and the sharp acidity that slices right through it leaving you angling for another sip. Quite long after-flavors. 92

Chapter 25
Rui Reguinga and Terrenus

Sub-region: Portalegre
Address: Ponte dos Olhos de Água, São Salvador da Aramenha, Marvão
Owner/winemaker: Rui Reguinga
Phone: (+351) 243 592 049
Email: terrenusveritae@gmail.com
Website: http://www.ruireguinga.com/en/

Over the last three decades Rui Reguinga has been a staunch champion of the cooler mountainous grape-growing region of Portalegre; its old, nearly abandoned, vineyards, and its local *talha* winemaking traditions. It is fitting that Reguinga has recently established his own adega just a hundred meters or so from the ruined 1st century Roman town of Ammaia. With its amphora and clay winemaking pots still intact, this historically important archaeological site anchors Portalegre's 'northern' *talha* culture in the ancient past just as Saõ Cucufate does for Southern Alentejo's *talha* culture.

Rui Reguinga amongst some of his old vines

Reguinga notes: 'Until the 1970s, most wine was made in *talha*s.' He mourns the corresponding sharp decline in local grape production. Around 400ha (1,000 acres) in its heyday, this slipped to 46ha (113 acres) by 1989 and has only recently returned to 622ha in 2020. Regardless of their diminished size, the surviving older vineyards are important preserves of local biodiversity and grape preferences as well as historical farming traditions.

It was providential that Reguinga began his first harvest at Portalegre's most venerable old estate, Tapada do Chaves, in 1991, with its magnificent 120-year-old vineyard. Since then the experience he gained throughout his career has reinforced his belief in the superiority of grapes produced from vines of this age.

A third-generation winemaker, Reguinga studied grape-growing at Lisbon Institute of Agronomy, followed by post-graduate winemaking studies at Portuguese Catholic University and Bordeaux University. He has made wine throughout a wide range of Portugal's main regions (Tejo, Dao, Douro, Madeira, Alentejo) and forayed far beyond into the greater world of wine: Argentina, Brazil, Sri Lanka, Australia, New Zealand, Bordeaux. The end result of all this has led to a breadth of winemaking experience with a variety of grape varieties grown under a wide range of cool and hot climatic conditions and soil types.

Reguinga sums up the advantages of this diverse career, 'I believe that the greater the experience a winemaker has outside the lands he knows, the greater his capacity to confront new situations. I began by being fascinated with the style of the New World but in the last years have returned to my origins.' Joni Mitchell summed up a similar sentiment once, 'you don't know what you got, till it's gone.'

Which sends me back to my first meeting with Rui Reguinga over a decade ago. He had taken me up a long and winding road near Porto da Espada in the Parque Natural da Serra de São Mamede. The destination, his pride and joy, a 90-year-old field blend vineyard named Vinha da Serra, that few at that point were interested in working, let alone owning. It clung tightly to a very steep slope (760m) just below the crest of the last ridge that stared off into the barren western plains of Spain. As we sat amongst the ancient vines, their battered old gnarly limbs, stunted from relentless wind, cold nights and even colder winters, my thoughts turned back to the special 'old vine' wine I'd drunk earlier at his adega. The hostile environment up there and the creaky old plants it produced were key to the tiny amounts of highly concentrated juice produced that made the wine so magical.

The key to understanding Reguinga's wine is understanding the primacy of the grapes that come from these old vineyards. The point is not letting winemaking get in the way of seeing those grapes as clearly as possible.

As a journeyman winemaker who long ago mastered the art of 'modern' technologically driven 'internationalist' wine styles and worked his way through all the trends and fads involved with them, he is now convinced that *talha* allow you to 'feel the strength and purity' of a wine more clearly: 'You find more minerality and freshness. You get the grapes as they are. You feel the greenness if unripe, which I like, because they aren't tempered by barrels. It shows the terroir and season much more.' For him 'barrels kill everything...aroma, complexity,' and so he's steadily moved away from that dominating influence.

After paying his dues as a contract winemaker Reguinga has finally achieved his 'dream...to have my own winery.' The new adega, overlooking Ammaia's ruins, was converted from a 1950s-era coffee-roasting factory, conveniently located close to Spain, 'so the coffee could be more easily smuggled across the border.' The winery isn't exclusively focused on *talha* wine, having a mix of small stainless steel tanks, a large, neutral wooden cone-shaped vessel, a biodynamic concrete egg, and Artenova's modern adaptation of a Roman *Dolium* fermentation pot from Tuscany. Each has a different role to play in his various old vine wines.

Terrenus has two *talha*. The newest (600 liter) is used for whites. It's dated 1859, produced and stamped by a master from the greatest northern center of *talha*-making in the 19th century, Campo Mayor. His reds have been made in a 2000-liter *talha* since 2014, which has since been transplanted to the new adega. Reguinga light-heartedly grumbles that they are 'not easy to move.'

Where previously his *talha* wines were reds, he has just made his first white. He experimented several years ago making an 'orange wine,' which used a three-month-long maceration and wasn't happy with the results. 'Maceration loses the freshness...you need to find the balance,' and that involves 'reading' each wine for its individuality. 'If there's too much maceration, it's not nice. Freshness is important,' continuing, 'I like the pure freshness of the grape.'

Having learned a lesson from too much orangeness, his new white *talha* wine, based on an old vine field blend, 'doesn't use so much maceration.' He added that keeping the wine in *talha* until November 11 is 'not easy' given Portalegre's cooler climate and later harvest dates.

His red is 'fermented in *talha* [certified after St. Martin's Day], then aged in smaller Artenova's amphora for 7-8 months.' It is interesting that Artenova's *Dolium*-shaped pots are remarkably similar to those in Ammaia's nearby museum.

'Buying old vineyards takes time. You have to develop a relationship with the owners,' Reguinga explains the trust and respect involved in any handover of stewardship. It's taken a while, but he has recently added two new 'old' vineyards alongside his original Vinha da Serra. Both are within a couple of kilometers (mile plus) of his adega.

The younger vineyard is named Vinha da Ammaia, a 60-year-old mixed field blend reserved for his *talha* wines: including whites Roupeiro, Arinto and Bical and reds Trincadeira, Moreto, and Castelão. The second is much older at 120 years, named Clos dos Muros, and includes: Gran Noir, Trincadeira, Aragonez, Moreto, Tinta Grossa, Alicante Bouschet, Castelão, Tinta Carvalha, Alfrocheiro, Corropio, and Tinta Francesa.

Of these, the last five reds plus whites, Arinto and Bical, are more common in north Alentejo blends than in south. They shape *talha* wine differently than those from further south.

Reguinga firmly believes that the combination of *talha* and local old vineyards is 'the new way' for Portalegre to reclaim its own distinctive future.

Rui Reguinga's collection of winemaking equipment

The Wines

Terrenus Vinha da Ammaia 1859 Amphora Branco 2022. A November 2022 sample bottled from *talha* for future reference. Ultra-fresh, lifted citrus (lemons, grapefruit) and tropical (passionfruit, pineapple) aromas with a touch of fresh vanilla bean. Quite aromatic. Perhaps a little higher alcohol this year? Very even tempered in the mouth, great balance, with lots of acidity driving forward motion. Flavors of tart peach, apricot and pear shaded with characters similar to aromatics. 95/10

Terrenus Vinha da Ammaia 1859 Amphora Branco 2021 12%. From a field blend of 60-year-old Arinto, Bical and Malvasia. A golden amber-colored wine, still very young in its lifespan. It offers up quite pronounced green stem and young plant leaf florals, outlined with spicier, apple-skin, peach-pit notes. Full-bodied and full-flavored, viscous in the mouth with fresh apricot and pit notes. Quite a big, powerful white with good length and structure following on with tart, stone-fruit juiciness through the finish. I would love to try it again in a year or two, assuming a great evolution. 93

Terrenus Vinha da Ammaia 1859 Amphora Tinto 2022. A November 2022 sample bottled from *talha* for future reference. As friendly as it is fresh, aromas leap from the glass full of black fruits (blackberries, currants, black cherries) and vanilla bean high tones. Sweetly ripe black fruits up front in the mouth, with great fruit depth, integration and fine, firm, tannins and crisp acidity in support. Again, looking forward to seeing how this wine evolves, but impressive now. 96

Terrenus Vinha da Ammaia 1859 Amphora Tinto 2021 14%. From a field blend of 60-year-old Trincadeira, a year on from birth and settling into itself, this offers up well integrated black cherry and chocolate, black forest gateau characters. Finely viscous with delineated acidity and fine, puckery tannins. An exciting wine that should drink well over next few years. A very clean, precise gastronomic style of wine, perfect for quaffing down with dinner, summertime or winter. 92

Terrenus Vinha da Ammaia Tinto 2018 13.5% Vinha do Talha DOC. Made from 60-year-old vines with predominant Trincadeira blended with Moreto and Castelao, fermented in large local *talha,* then shifted after St. Martin's Day for 6 month maturation in 600 liter modern, Roman-inspired Dolium-shaped pots made by Artenova near Florence. Mix of dried herb and red fruit notes, with emphasis on freshness, acidity and aromas. Fine, tight tannins and long clean, juicy finish. Nice wine, which should continue to evolve positively. 93-94

Terrenus Tinto Amphora 2014 13.5%. His first *talha* wine, but not able to be certified because his adega was outside the DOC then, even though it was kept in *talha* until St. Martin's Day. This wine has more Trincadeira with less Moreto and Castelao. Still fresh and lively, with similar herbal red fruit aromas. A little denser, and slicker textured with similar tannins and acidity. With maturation it's softer, more integrated now. 91

Chapter 26
Susana Esteban

Sub-region: Portalegre
Address: Quinta das Sesmarias 7300-000 Alegrete, Serra de São Mamede, Portalegre
Owner/Winemaker: Susana Esteban
Email: enologia@susanaesteban.com
Website: https://www.susanaesteban.com/en/home
Vineyard names: Saio Frio is an 85 year old, mixed white variety vineyard,, Sesmarias?
Talha: 3 (700, 750 & 800 liters) Other vessels: 2 oak foudres (1100, 800 liters No *pés* use

Susana Esteban's story is very much about old grape varieties, old vines and wedding these to clay pot winemaking.

Originally from Spain's cool, wet Galicia region, she searched northern Alentejo for three years for the perfect place to grow and make the kind of wines she has always wanted to craft. Eventually she settled on a site in one of its cooler parts, a little east of Portalegre on the southern slopes of its adjacent Serra de São Mamede mountains.

Susana Esteban in her tasting room near Alegrete

The new vineyard site lies below the impressive hilltop castle town of Alegrete and sits astride the southern slope of a natural wilderness preserve. Occupying a semi-derelict, over 400-year-old olive grove, Esteban left the older trees in place mixed within the vineyard following traditional practices 'as in the old days', while replanting the younger 200-year-old trees to border a boulevard-like road up its centre. This new vineyard is very much connected to the past.

An important draw for her was proximity to a favorite 85-year-old, field blended vineyard, Saio Frio, from which she has been sourcing grapes since 2011. Back in the day, she used to search out tiny pockets of old vines, calling on the owners to negotiate access to their grapes. Now they call her. Saio Frio contains around 20 white varieties -

several of which remain unidentified. As of 2022, Esteban is in the process of replicating this vineyard by carefully transplanting individual cuttings, vine for vine, into her new vineyard.

Modern fitout built on an old adega

Not minding that she doesn't know exactly what grapes are being replanted, selection is based on the health and quality of each plant. Her only concern is to maintain this old vineyard's biodiversity and high-quality fruit, ensuring the old vineyard's DNA will live on while maintaining a source of fruit similar to what she has been using for years.

Her vineyard site is relatively cooler than most of Alentejo because of its high altitude at 700 meters/yards. More similar to the Dao region to the north, its diurnal temperature shifts between 28C-degree days down to 14C degrees at night in August, guaranteeing higher natural acidity. Where most of Alentejo harvests in August, her vineyard begins significantly later in early September.

Estebans's winemaking pedigree is impressive. After having earned a Chemistry degree from Santiago de Compostela University and then a Masters in Enology at La Rioja University, she has since worked as winemaker for two top Douro adegas, Quinta do Côtto and Quinta do Crasto, as well as consulting for several Alentejo producers and picking up several wine-making awards in the process.

Not unlike Rui Reguenga's long history of consultancy, much of her previous working life was based around 'modern' conventional, technologically driven winemaking. But now she is free to create her own project, she is making the kind of wine she wants to make, which is less technologically driven, leaning more towards traditional, local practices. Esteban's winemaking style focuses on elegance and seeks to preserve the identity of her vineyards. In brief, it is about the fruit produced and, ultimately, the way it is shaped by clay.

That said, she is not strictly following the traditional *talha* white-wine formula. Her approach is more a pragmatic mix of old and new. Aiming for more freshness and fruit purity, juice is pressed off the grapes before fermenting in *talha*, to avoid the tannins produced by the DOC's required extended skin contact. Nor does she rigidly follow the St. Martin's Day deadline. She also inserts stainless steel tubes into *talha* to reduce and control fermentation temperatures more along lines of conventional 'modern' stainless steel fermentation. And so her wines don't carry Vinhos de Talha DOC certification.

Her interest in *talha* is more for its internal convection currents and the natural battonage produced by the shape of inside walls, along with its neutrality and oxygen transfer rate, similar to barrel fermentation and maturation. She believes this provides the advantages of oak fermentation without any negatively intrusive oak characters: aromas, flavors, tannins, etc.

Esteban's first *talha*-produced wine style, Procura na Ânfora, was born from this approach.

And then something unexpected happened. In 2019, Covid forced a change in processing, which, along with distinct weather conditions, created an entirely new wine style. Experimenting that year, her Procura used 30% skin contact, which she worked in three *talhas* like a red wine. She kept the wine on the skins until January, intending to then bottle it. But at that point, she felt skin tannins were still too pronounced, and so she returned the wine to the *talha* for ageing to refine and soften its tannic structure.

Covid forced her to defer any bottling until July, by which time cellar temperatures had increased beyond all previous conditions. That warmth, in turn, caused a flor to develop, similar to the carpet of yeast that forms on top of Fino Sherry, bringing with it flor's distinctive floral-saline aroma.

Obviously it wasn't 'Procura' anymore. But she liked its accidental complexity and unexpected distinctiveness. The wine's uniqueness was derived from long skin contact, Alentejan grapes, and the flor and *talha* created textures, all at a low 12% alcohol. Nothing like barrique-produced Sherry at 15%, nor characters previously found in *talha* wine for that matter. She dubbed this lighter, finer form of Portuguese 'Fino' Tira O Veu meaning 'veil of flowers.'

Unexpectedly, although the cellar temperatures were cooler, she reproduced the style in 2020. This time the flor developed spontaneously, but earlier in November, likely because the flor probably now inhabits the *talha*. These characters now belong to her wines alone, not replicable by anyone else, anywhere else.

So the current plan is to continue making Tira O Veu in a flor-infused cellar on one side of the adega, separating this from a new flor-free cellar on the other side, where the original Procura na Anfora style will continue to be made. Her new adega has been built on the shell of an old adega, which Susana has transformed into a light and airy white-washed space, with remnants of old wine-making equipment placed like works of art.

Susana's story is a testament to how a new approach, reconceiving ancient *talha* technology, can spin off entirely new forms of wine beyond anyone's wildest imagination.

White wines

Susana Esteban Tira O Veu Vinhas Velas 2022 12.5?%. Fresh from Amphora, drawn on St Martins Day 2022. Presents delicate white blossom, elderflower and white pepper notes, counter-pointing savory mineral aromas. Right up front, it offers very pure, sweetly ripe, crisp, fresh pear fruit characters. Full bodied, flavor-filled textures are infused with fruit that gradually taper off into a fine finish. Citrus acidity and pear fruits hang on tongue, lasting well beyond swallowing. Lovely, elegant, refreshing, all in one go. Somewhat reminiscent of Alvarinho, but more multi-dimensional. Old, mixed vine field blend, grown at cooler high altitudes strutting their stuff. 92

Susana Esteban Tira O Veu Vinhas Velas 2021 12.5%. Compared to the younger 2022, this old vine wine shows a savory development shifting towards green plant, green veggie shadings of baseline minerality. It retains white fruit flavors, although less fresh, more minerally and neutral. Textures are less plush, tighter, more condensed nice spicy crispness on the tail end of this wine. Rounds out with airing, retaining a tightly balanced acidity. Long after-flavors. More concentrated than 2022, but tighter, more nervy than 2020, less voluptuous or concentrated. 95

Procura na Anfora 2022 12.5?%. From the 85-year-old Saio Frio vineyard, a mixed field blend of more than 20 varieties. This hybrid style is fermented in *talha* but removed quickly to avoid dominating skin tannins from extended contact. This St Martins Day 2022 sample, taken directly from *talha*, is as good as previous vintages and should evolve along the same lines. Newborn as it is, it sings loudly with ultra-fresh green melon, pear, flower stem and blossom aromas, and hums along in the mouth with similar fruit characters. Deeply concentrated, densely texture and ever so viscous, it delivers remarkable flavor length that last well over a minute after swallowing. I loved its meltaway finish, exquisite balance and finesse. A remarkable wine from a great old vineyard. 97

Procura na Anfora 2018 12.5%. From the 85-year-old Saio Frio vineyard, a mixed field blend of more than 20 varieties. This hybrid style is fermented in *talha* but removed quickly to avoid dominating skin tannins from extended contact. I first tasted this wine in November at Amphora Day 2019 when it was still fresh as a daisy. Then it was packed full of lovely fresh green stem florals, spice and fresh green grape/fruit aromas. Fine, clean and smooth as glass in the mouth with textures laced with mineral flavors and an intriguing touch of spearmint spiciness. Amazing flavor length, it was a wine with great poise and elegance. Tasted again in November of 2021, It remains remarkably aromatic, highly concentrated, minerally from start to finish with fine acidity and great length. Great wine. 96-98/100

Esteban Procura na Anfora 2017 12.5%. Extraordinarily fresh for four-year-old white from amphora. Minerally driven characters with pear, white peach and grape aromas with hints of flowers behind. Markedly integrated, rounded and fleshy, with a deeply viscous, plush texture laden with white fruits and juicy acidity propelling flavor length. Touch of sweet fruitiness on finish. Very long. Distinctive. Tasted 1.22 96

Susana Esteban Tira O Veu 2019 13%. Originally intended as Procura na Anfora 2019 but Covid delayed bottling and flor yeast took hold reshaping the wine. And so it became 'Veil of Flowers' instead. A very light yellow/green curious sort of 'orange' wine with a Jerez flavor. Opening with slightly buttery, green stem aromas and flavors, underpinned by subtle fino floral-saline characters. In the mouth it offers a full rich texture cut through with fine skin tannins, ample acidity and ends with a sappy, juicy finish. Tasting this in November 2021, I recall tasting it as an experimental sample first at Amphora Day 2019 with 50% skin contact. Back then it was full of fresh quince and apple skin aromas.

Susana Esteban Tira O Veu 2020 12%. An intentional 2nd edition of this interesting hybrid style, where *talha* skin contact meets flor yeast influence. Susana likes this even more than the 2019, for its 'spontaneity and more graceful outcome.' Employing 30% skin contact and then awaiting flor development, the wine differs in being bottled earlier after 8 months. Beautifully integrated aromas given its youthful development, its texture is laced with subtle flor, saline notes. Slick, full, fleshy, continuous, it ends with a very long tapered, meltaway finish. An extraordinary wine. 98

Susana Esteban's *talha* and wine (image provided by Susana Esteban)

Chapter 27
Adega Cooperativa Vidigueira, Cuba and Alvito

Sub-region: Vidigueira
Address: Bairro Industrial, 7960-305 Vidigueira, Portugal
Chairman José Miguel Almeida
Winemaker: Vasco Fernandes
Marketing: danielaalmeida@adegavidigueira.pt
Phone: (+351) 284 437 240
Email: loja@adegavidigueira.pt
Website: https://adegavidigueira.pt/en/
General Information: The cooperative's *pés* is exclusively 100% beeswax
Good coop *talha* making link: https://casadastalhas.adegavidigueira.pt/vinho-de-talha/?lang=en

Founded in 1960, the Adega Cooperativa Vidigueira, Cuba and Alvito's 300 members farm 15,000 hectares and produce nearly five million bottles of wine a year. Few realize that Adega Vidigueira contains the largest vestige of family-based *talha* winemaking culture. And while the 2000 bottles of Vinho de Talha DOC that Adega Vidigueira makes each year is a minuscule fraction of their conventionally produced wine, it is significant in many other respects.

Display of *talha* at Adega Vidigueira

The Cooperative's chairman José Miguel Almeida played a central role in the resuscitation of *talha* culture in the middle 1990s. Joining the seminal Vide Frades Project in 1997, he was president for 10 years during the important period when Vinho de Talha DOC rules were being developed within Alentejo's governing CVR organization. Following on from that, Adega Vidigueira produced the first certified bottling of Vinho de Talha wine - a point of great pride.

In support of all this, the Cooperative actively celebrates its *talha* heritage through a purposefully built interpretive center: Casa das Talhas. The center includes a couple of working *talhas*, a tasting room and a gathering space. The main 'working' *talha* cellar, across a courtyard, is in the process of moving into a beautifully restored, centuries old cellar. During a recent visit, a busload of children from the local school were enthusiastically stomping grapes destined to fill the first *talha* of the new vintage - the best sort of living history lesson.

José Miguel Almeida with one of his *talha*-shaped bottles

Although the Coop prides itself on preserving and encouraging traditional local *talha* wine culture, it also, inadvertently, played a major role in its historical decline. During the 20th century, the life of a small vineyard owner and tiny winemaker would have been difficult. Growing and making and selling, let alone marketing and distributing to a wider audience, would have produced a marginal, if not precarious income even at the best of times.

When the Cooperative was formed in 1960, it offered growers economies of scale, technological security and a steady income, allowing the *talha* wine sellers to focus on growing grapes, and dispensing with all the more 'iffy' parts of the wine equation: making, selling, marketing, and distribution. So it is little wonder that where there were once hundreds of individual local *talha* winemakers, suddenly they flowed, en-masse, to cooperative production.

This in turn meant that families had the option to retain a small pot or two for family consumption or to reclaim newly emptied cellar space for living room. Undoubtedly there was a steam roller effect from this, as the remaining *talha* producers would have been undercut and forced out of business by cheaper, more modern styles of Coop wine. Such is the inevitable flow of 'progress.'

By the 1990s *talha* winemaking teetered on the edge of extinction, barely kept alive by a handful of people and their living memories of what had been. The recognition of this loss energized some in the community to reclaim their heritage, inspiring the initial activism that eventually established the Vinho de Talha DOC certification and the elevation of these wines to a special status within current production.

The Coop's single 'Centenaria' Vinho de Talha DOC is unique in being made exclusively from century-old vines. One can't understate how important it is to commercialize - thus creating an incentive to preserve - these old, field blended, bush-vine vineyards with their seemingly haphazard mixture of many varieties. Several of these are not only unique to the area, but dangerously on the edge of extinction.

José Miguel Almeida took me to one of these tiny vineyards that was at least 100 years old (perhaps 130 or more). Growing in sandy, highly infertile soil, what was so striking was how the vineyard had survived in such a hostile setting. Whereas other old vineyards I've visited around the globe had large, thigh-sized, gnarly trunks, these vines were as gnarly, but considerably finer, more wrist-like, indicating very slow, stifled growth.

Very old vines planted the ancient way...amongst the olive trees

Another indication of their antiquity was evidence of *merguila* (to put in soil) technique. In the past this was a common way to avoid costly new cuttings of grafted vines. Instead, branches of existing vines were buried, which then re-rooted, establishing new vines. Snake-like, these new vines plunge in and out of the ground, looking like the

Loch Ness Monster. Further evidence of ancient farming practices were olive trees – clearly hundreds (maybe thousands) of years old – inter-planted helter skelter within the vineyard.

The vines included many ancient, local white varieties common within the Coop's borders: Antão Vaz, Roupeiro, Mantuedo, Diagalves, Larião, Perrum and many others. Almeida mentioned that several are yet to be identified and likely to be distinct new discoveries of ancient unknown vines. And, like the exceedingly rare Larião, tottering on the verge of extinction. Many of the grapes have a wide range of DNA mutations indicating they either originated locally or have been growing there a long, long time. Science reinforces the old local belief that Antão Vaz is the 'Vidigueira grape variety'.

Within walking distance of Saõ Cucufate, all this begs an intriguing question, going back a few thousand years. What came first, Cucufate and the grapes it left behind or - noting that the name Vidigueira has its origin in the word 'videira' (vine) - was it the existing local grapes that attracted Cucufate's construction?

This small plot is only one of many the Cooperative preserves within its corporate body of growers. These are some of the oldest vineyards, not just in Alentejo, but in all of Iberia. Many of these vineyards are too tiny to produce even a barrel of wine, but collectively they create a huge and powerful body of old local vines, endangered biodiversity and unlimited potential to make distinctive, highly concentrated wine, and in quantities perfectly suited to *talha* production.

My one criticism of Adega Vidigueira's Vinho de Talha DOC wine is its low price. Between the high labor costs required to preserve quality and the endangered nature of its rare vineyards, financial rewards need to support the obvious value of the time and effort in growing the grapes and making the wine. Given its hand-made nature, use of rare, old, low yielding, highly concentrated grapes and the wine's notable high quality, this wine should be selling at a premium price.

One the other hand, one also has to respect the Coop's preference to sell the wine for a price members can readily afford. It's hard to criticize their choice of 'love over gold'.

Perhaps a happy compromise will find its way to a solution. The Coop is blessed not only with a number of century plus vineyards, but many old vines from 40 years up to that magical 100-year mark. It also has plenty of cellar space and many unused *talha* to raise production well above its current 2000-bottle production. I reckon there is plenty of room for a wide range of tiered branding levels able to satisfy a range of wallet sizes: Centurion, Vinhas Muito Velhas and Vinhas Velhas Vinho de Talha DOC.

I'd most certainly take a bottle of all three.

The wines

Cooperativa Vidigueira Talha Branco 2022 13%. Destined for Vinho de Talha DOC certification, this blend of Antão Vaz, Roupeiro, Mantuedo, Diagalves, Larião, Perrum and others… is sourced only from century old vines. Only 600 litres produced this year. Fresh from *talha* on St. Martins Day, the wine shows lovely florals with a touch of white pepper aromas. Another fine, elegantly-styled wine underpriced for its quality. 93/100

Cooperativa Vidigueira Talha Branco 2021 13%. Vinho de Talha DOC certification. Another highly concentrated blend of Antão Vaz, Roupeiro, Mantuedo, Diagalves, Larião, Perrum and others… sourced only from century-old vines. This year is showing an interesting toasty, nutty, roasted corn-like bottle development reminiscent of Australian Riesling. Finely textured with lemony acidity and integrated skin tannins. 90

Cooperativa Vidigueira Talha Palhete 2022. Destined for Vinho de Talha DOC certification, this co-fermented mix of red and white grapes comes from 100+ year old vines. Only 600 litres of this traditional 'peoples' wine is made, prized for its fresh strawberry aromas, soft texture and gluggability. 88

Cooperativa Vidigueira Talha 2020 13% .A highly concentrated blend of Antão Vaz, Roupeiro, Mantuedo, Diagalves, Larião, Perrum and others… sourced only from 80-130+ year-old vines. Super balance and integration throughout this wine, with delicate flower stem aromas and subtle pickled lemon flavors shading pervasive minerality throughout. A bargain that should sell for 3 times its price. 93

Cooperativa Videgueira Vinho de Talha 2018 12.5%. Tasted after a couple of years of maturity with no signs of oxidation. Floral and fruit characters have evolved into interesting butter and green tea characters. Texture has fleshed out with a degree of viscosity and fine acidity. Nice gastronomic wine. 89

Chapter 28
XXVI Talhas

Sub-region: Vidigueira
Address: Adega Mestre Daniel, 64X2+96 Vila Alva, Portugal
Owners: Genoveva Santos, Daniel Parreira, Alda and Samuel Pernicha, Ricardo Santos
Winemaker: Ricardo Santos
Email: info.xxvi.talhas@gmail.com
Website: https://en.xxvi-talhas.pt/
Association of Vinho de Talha Producers (APVT)

My first visit to XXVI Talhas was a revelation. It was like unlocking the door to a winery that had been frozen in time for the last half-century. Now, here it was open for business once again, seemingly without having skipped a beat.

Inside Adega Mestre Daniel

That, of course, belies the fact that a lot of careful restoration and scrubbing up has taken place to achieve this state.

This was down to a group of four childhood friends born and raised in Vila Alva: Daniel Parreira, his sister Alda, cousin Samuel Pernicha, and Ricardo Santos. Daniel and Alda's grandfather, Daniel António Tabaquinho dos Santos, was a master winemaker who made *talha* wine in Adega Mestre Daniel until his death in 1985. Reopening Adega Mestre Daniel in 2018, the friends began revitalising twenty-six *talha* that had been sitting empty and fallow since Mestre Daniel's death. Hence the name XXVI Talhas.

Currently the four commute on weekends from Lisbon, where they all live and work. Daniel and Alda's mother, Genoveva Santos, still owns her father's adega, but it's clear the project is a cooperative effort with everyone; extended family, friends and all, playing the best role they can, with Daniel project-managing, Alda and Samuel handling communications, and Ricardo working as senior enologist. Ricardo's father, João Manuel Santos, handles the

Daniel Parreira, his sister Alda, Ricardo Santos, and Samuel Pernicha (image provided by XXVI Talha)

day-to-day winemaking in Vila Alva. In his childhood João helped Mestre Daniel at the adega, providing an important link back to unlocking *talha* wine secrets.

On another level, the project is greater than just *talha* wine. All are deeply committed to revitalising their little village (population 400) which has been losing population for decades. It's sad to know that in 1950 Vila Alva had reached its peak of 1300 people with over 70 small and medium sized wineries and almost every household had a small *talha* (*tareco*) opened on St. Martin's Day, supplying family needs through to the next vintage.

But all has not been lost. Much of Vila Alva's *talha* culture still remains hidden behind doors, like Adega Mestre Daniel, patiently waiting to come alive again.

Currently there are at least eight adegas with over 130 *talhas*, still producing wine, and another fourteen adegas with over 86 unused *talhas* behind locked doors, many of which could return to production. This, of course, compares with the hundreds more that existed pre-20th century, when vineyard totals steadily shrank from 1200 down to present 400 hectares, but it offers up hope for the future.

Indeed, while at XXVI, a 30-something friend from a couple of doors up the road invited me to have a look at his future project. After unlocking a large door there stood another twenty large *talhas* sitting, dust-covered and unused, 'involuntarily mothballed' just as Adega Mestre Daniel's had been (see Potted History section). The team at XXVI Talhas are clearly an infectious lot.

Adega Mestre Daniel's twenty-six *talhas* range from 300 to 1300 liters, some dating from the 19th century. Most are made of clay, but four are made of reinforced cement, manufactured by local Vila Alva masters in the 1930s (see Talha Terroir section).

Winemaker Ricardo explained that each *talha* has its own dynamics with size and shape producing different wine from the same grape source. In particular, neck, collar and shoulder size and body shape determine how punch-down of the cap is dealt with, and, each factor in turn also creates different vectors for internal flow of currents within the *talha's* belly from top to bottom.

XXVI use traditional *pés*. Luckily, during my visit I experienced the first time the adega team applied *pés* to two of its larger 1300-liter *talha*. Feeling confident after successfully applying *pés* to a smaller 600-liter-*talha*, nine men gathered to lower seriously heavy, man-sized pots from their normal standing position. These were rolled across a floor, re-raised, head first, over a fire. After a couple of hours heating and deemed hot enough to absorb the wax, they were flipped back over and lowered down again. Resting on their bellies, they were coated internally with beeswax and pine resin, and finally repositioned into the original space ready for filling. (see To *Pés* or not to *Pés*).

It was a smoky five-hour process involving lots of grunting, near loss of control, a fair bit of dodging, coughing, tears and triumphant cheers - nothing short of a jaw-dropping, sometimes breathtaking, experience to watch. The striking thing about this relatively rare, recently resurrected process, is it was once commonly repeated hundreds of times every year throughout this part of Alentejo, going back not just hundreds, but thousands of years.

Because XXVI Talhas are focused 'on stimulating the local economy and the traditional vine growing', all the grapes come from within the Vila Alva parish. Vineyards are field blends of mixed varieties with vines aged between 25 and 50 years old. Sourced from family, friends or neighbors, all are grown without irrigation.

Vines to the southeast (between Vila Alva and Vidigueira) are planted in granitic soils and the northwestern vineyards are planted in schist soils. The two completely different soil types and micro-climates offer up some interesting fruit choices to play around with and carefully match to differing *talha* types and sizes.

White varieties are mainly Antão Vaz, Roupeiro, Mantuedo, Perrum, Diagalves, Larião, Roupeiro and others. Diagalves & Mantuedo varieties were often the latest to ripen in the past, which has become an advantage now with global warming. Red grapes revolve around Trincadeira, Roriz and, most especially, Tinto Grossa. Ricardo mentioned that Tinta Grossa has a strong local story, where villagers in Vila Alva call it 'our grape' because of its dominance there. Indications so far suggest it has a high clonal biodiversity locally, suggesting it has lived there a very long time.

XXVI Talhas have three main wine styles. 'Do Tareco' follows the classic *talha* process of fermentation on skins for a couple of months, completed on Saint Martin's Day (11 November), then bottled immediately to keep it light and fresh for drinking over the coming months.

Their mainline 'Mestre Daniel' also follows the St. Martin's day formula, but a selection is made of the best *talhas* and the wine is kept on the 'mother' until February or March of the following year, aiming for more complexity and skin derived structure.

The adega's reserve is a special numbered 'Single *talha*' wine made only in one pot using the best grapes coming entirely from a single old vineyard. Produced only from a top vintage and held on 'mother' for 5 or 6 months before bottling, production is usually around 1000 bottles. Similar to Herdade do Rocim's Jupiter, the point is to bottle the ultimate in terroir: grapes coming from a specific plot and season, then vinified within a highly specific clay container and matured within its parameters.

XXVI also produce a little 'Palhete', a very traditional local style, that co-ferments a mixture of white and red grapes, resulting in wine somewhere between a rose and light red. Although strictly speaking mixing red and whites is not officially allowed by EU or local appellation regulations, it is nevertheless an important traditional style worth continuing. It bridges back to a time when *talha* was thriving in Vila Alva and people enjoyed the blend of red and whites that were growing together in their vineyards; something lighter and fresher than a red, and fuller and richer than a white. While a bit of an outlaw within a world of top-down regulation, there is a growing movement, from the bottom up, to bring back this people's style of wine.

All in all, XXVI Talhas are a force to be reckoned with. The adega is a hive of innovative creativity, buzzing with youthful energy and ever focused on returning their community to the prosperity and happy times it once had in the past. One can only expect even better things to come.

White Wines

XXVI Titan do Tareco Branco 2021 11.5%. Named after the small family sized *talhas* called *tarecos*. Lots of fresh pear, spicy white grape and applesauce aromas and flavors here. Soft textured and full-bodied with dense fruit you can roll around in your mouth, and decent flavor length. A lovely, eminently quaffable wine for everybody. Modern Vinho de Talha style that delivers on all fronts. 90/100

XXVI Talhas Mestre Daniel Branco 2021 12% Vinho de Talha DOC. A blend of mostly Antão Vaz, Perrum and Rupeiro. Honeyed mineral aromas initially, followed by condensed and concentrated, multi-layered textures underpinned by very fine skin tannins with just enough gentle acidity to balance beautifully. With airing it develops fresher flower stem aromas and blossom notes, and white grape flavors emerge. Quite complex wine that needs time and oxygen to unfold. 93

XXVI Talhas Mestre Daniel Branco Talha X 2021 11.5% Vinho de Talha DOC. As before, a blend of Antão Vaz, Diagalves, Perrum, Rupeiro, Mantuedo, others from a single parcel of old mixed field blend of pure white varieties planted mid-century. Offers up lovely mix of spicy florals and honeyed bees wax, similar flavors in nicely concentrated texture with fine skin tannins in support. Terrific on the finish, terrific wine. 91

XXVI Talhas Do Tareco Branco 2020 12% Vinho de Talha DOC. Mainly from Antão Vaz that wears a bright golden yellow color. Apple skin, fresh cider aromas and flavors, follow through a slick, continuous texture. Interesting visceral notes with a touch of fine skin tannins locking in alongside firm acidity. Good flavor length. Bear in mind that traditionally this style of everyday quaffing wine was meant to be consumed within months after fermentation; by late 2021 it had reached a later stage in development than it probably ever would have in the past. With airing it seemed to freshen up, becoming much more floral, less cider-like and its texture blossomed with a mix of viscous fruit, nicely balanced by a touch of acidity with very fine tannins. Tasted Sept 2021. 88

XXVI Talhas Mestre Daniel Branco 2019 13% Vinho de Talha DOC. A blend of mostly Antão Vaz, Perrum and Rupeiro. A step up in quality, this is darker and more golden than Tareco. Similarly it offers stronger, more dense aromas of apple skins, flower stems, cooked pears, with similar flavors. Denser and more concentrated in the mouth, it carries an edgier structure with more skin tannins and acidity powering length of flavor. A much more gastronomic style, less refreshing than the Tareco. It cut through grilled tuna perfectly. 24 hours later, it developed a honeyed marmalada (Portuguese version made with quince fruit), like carmelized citrus/orange) character and deeper, darker shaded fruitiness. 89

XXVI Talhas Mestre Daniel Branco Talha X 2019 11.5% Vinho de Talha DOC. A blend of Antão Vaz, Diagalves, Perrum, Rupeiro, Mantuedo, others from a single parcel of old mixed field blend of pure white varieties planted mid-century. Deep amber colored. Spicy apricot pit and orange skin aromas. A visceral wine with skin tannins and acidic structure felt throughout. Impressively concentrated without thickness, finely balanced wine. Somewhere between an orange wine and Tareco. Fruit evolution is in keeping with the Tareco 2020, just denser, more compacted and longer. If you close your eyes, you can almost imagine it to be a red wine. 94

Red Wines

XXVI Talhas Mestre Daniel Tinto 2021 12.5% Vinho de Talha DOC. A blend of Trincadeira, Roriz, Tinto Grossa. Initially the nose displays a predominant savory minerality over a bedrock of blackfruit characters. With airing, aromas add a spicy red fruit floral component. Flavors mix red and blackfruits driven forward by lively acidity and a lashing of fine tannins that coat the tongue steadily creeping their way up onto the lips. Expansive, flavor-filled and long-finishing, this is a really impressively made wine. With continued airing the Tinta Grossa really makes its mark, shifting flavors toward the red cherry realm that increasingly takes on a graphite sheen as well. Although remarkably young, this wine suggests it will develop increasing greater degrees of elegance and refinement after further bottle age. Lucky are those who will have that opportunity. 96

XXVI Talhas Do Tareco Tinto 2020 13%. Full of fresh red fruit aromas and flavors, primarily red cherries with strawberries/raspberries behind. Juicy through to the finish, it feels like a young Beaujolais, still fresh and bouncy a year on. Structured more by fresh acidity than tannic bite. After airing, wine develops wild brambly fruits, quite sweetly-ripe ones. Here's the surprise. Initially this wine was too fruity and fresh for my tastes, but after it was open for 24 hours I really enjoyed it with dinner. The up front fruits had dialled back the fresh, brambliness into a more restrained savory cherry character, and I noticed it was a lot longer finishing wine. And had the most interesting tart aged-cherry flavors welling up on finish. 90

XXVI Talhas Mestre Daniel Tinto 2019 13% Vinho de Talha DOC. A blend of Trincadeira, Roriz, Tinto Grossa that offered up a blend of mineral and black fruit aromas initially. Rounded and soft entry into the mouth, tons of complex mix of black and red fruits, underpinned by fine tannins and acidity. 92

XXVI Talhas Mestre Daniel Tinto Talha XV 2019 14% Vinho de Talha DOC. From an old mixed vineyard primarily made up of Tinta Grossa grapes. Initially quite tight and closed down, offering reductive savory notes at best. With airing it quickly becomes broadly floral, developing a mixture of dried and fresh cherries with little hints of blueberries mixed in for added complexity. Tight and hard feeling initially, this fleshes out into a fullish body with a seamless mouthfeel driven forward by a nicely structured blend of fine tannins and juicy acidity. A really interesting, relatively unknown, grape variety that works as well as a single varietal as in a blend. 94

Traditional styles

XXVI Talhas Palhete do Tareco 2020 12.5%. A traditional everyday 'claret' style wine that blends and ferments white and grapes together in a *talha*. Intensely fruity nose full of strawberries and cherry characters, soft and welcoming and just as fruity in the mouth, with enough acidity to keep it all fresh. 88

XXVI Talha

PART 3: FOR THE WINE TOURIST

by Jennifer Mortimer

On the road to São Cucufate

Chapter 29
A Brief History of Alentejo

On the first day of our research trip to Alentejo in August 2021, it was hot - far too hot for applying *pés*, so we had a whole afternoon to wait before we could visit XXVI Talhas to watch the *pesage* of two of their *talha*. Paul decided to show me a very famous wine estate just west of Vidigueira.

We pulled in and parked the car. At the gate, the keeper eyed our credentials somewhat dubiously, but let us enter. Apart from a tiny black kitten warming itself on the hot cobblestones that skittered away as we approached, the place was empty. Shadowed by the cat, we trod the path up a small hill.

At the top of the rise, we came to an elegant standalone building; a meeting room, or a temple to the old gods, perhaps? We skirted to one side, and suddenly, there it was.

To the left, a grand swimming pool, and to the right, the winery, with its crusher and storage system, framed by thousand-year-old olive trees. Beyond lay the main accommodation block, a grand two-storeyed affair, built in contrasting layers of large grey stones and thin red terracotta bricks.

We passed alongside the pool, and entered through the entrance on the far side. The reception area was made of adjoining coved-ceilinged rooms, and adorned with paintings of angels playing music. One angel plays a *bajon*, precursor to the bassoon. Another, a medieval fiddle, still another, a Renaissance era cornet. Clearly, these paintings were not of the building's original era.

We walked on through to the inner chambers, past rooms where wine had once been stored in terracotta pots. A long gallery stretched down the building, edged with a handsome terrace overlooking the pool. At the end of the gallery, we climbed the staircase to the roof terrace, and were able to admire the view in a full 360 degrees.

It was breath-taking. It was completely deserted. And, it was in ruins.

This was Villa Aurica, also known as São Cucufate: the largest, most intact Roman ruin in the Iberian peninsula, and an iconic example of the evolution of the Alentejo wine estate over the millennia.

Villa Aurica started life in the 1st century as a Roman agricultural farm, the center of a small community, with the Roman (rich foreigner) owner's residence, and production and storage spaces for two of life's most important ingredients: wine and olive oil. There may have been some accommodation for domestics, but the (poor local) workers would likely have lived a little further away, in local villages such as Vila de Frades.

Appropriately, the Romans named the area now known as Portugal, 'Lusitania' after Lusus, the son of the Roman god of wine Bacchus. The people of the region were known as Lusitanians. They certainly drank wine; and archeological and literature studies also indicate that wine was being made in that part of Portugal for at least two thousand years before the Romans showed up.

We know that wine was being made at Villa Aurica in the Roman times because of 20th century archeological efforts into the São Cucufate ruins undertaken by the Portuguese authorities. These investigations discovered ancient grape seeds as well as weights of a type known to be used for pressing grapes.

We know that the wine was stored in terracotta pots because of the additional discovery of *dolium*-type storage fragments; '*dolium*' being the name given to the original Roman terracotta pot, the precursor to the *talha*.

It is thought that the Romans would make the wine in their Iberian estates, store the wine in large storage *dolia*, and then, when the wine was ready, it would be transferred into long, thin, handled amphora that were fixed inside ships, and transported via the Mediterranean sea to that epoch's most important export market: Rome.

Over the next few centuries, the main house was progressively expanded. The first renovation, in the 2nd century, appears to have been a modest expansion of the residence, perhaps the Roman owner seeking to stamp their own mark on the property, and making it more comfortable for their regular vacation-style visits.

São Cucufate: temple in the foreground, pool to the left, estate in the distance

The second, in the middle of the 4th century, represented a major rebuild, in a grand style, with a lengthy principal façade oriented around several interior courtyards, reflecting an opulence desired by Roman society. The nearby hills of Estremoz may have provided marble to line the floors and the walls. An extensive Roman baths complex was started.

But by 400 AD Rome was struggling under the weight of its giant empire and that extravagant era was about to come to an end. The bath complex was never completed. Perhaps the Roman owners over-reached their finances, or perhaps some other event caused them to give up on their grand design. Whichever, archaeology indicates that the villa was abandoned in the early-mid 5th century AD, and Rome itself finally fell in 476 AD.

Over the next few centuries Lusitania encountered waves of invasions, first by the Christian Visigoths and then by the Moors. Little is known about Villa Aurica's fate, until around the 9th century, when a convent dedicated to São Cucufate was established on the ruins of the villa; giving the property the name it is now known by.

Battles between the Christians and the Moors continued, until by the mid-13th century the Moors were largely defeated, and in 1255, 'Portugal' emerged as a country, with Lisbon as its capital. Around that time, the monastery of São Vicente de Fora took over control of São Cucufate, and the collection of buildings and fields became home to first Augustine and then Benedictine monks, both known for their winemaking skills.

References from that time mention wine production, so we can be confident that the art of winemaking continued in São Cucufate. Certainly the Catholic church needed a steady supply of wine for religious services - the taking of 'communion', which throughout Europe had led to Christian monks becoming major producers of wine. As Paul notes earlier, the Portuguese term 'tinto' for red wine came from the practice of 'tinting' the more prevalent supplies of white wine with red wine, as communion wine is expected to be red, like the blood of Christ it represented.

By the 1400s, Portugal was one of the richest countries in the world. The Portuguese sailed the seas in all directions, adventuring, trading, and colonizing. One of the most famous of the seafarers was Vasco de Gama, the first European to reach India by sea around the cape of Good Hope. De Gama was made the first count of Vidigueira in 1519. One might picture de Gama visiting São Cucufate, perhaps to sample their wine and buy some to take with him for drinking later. We hope this was the case, and not that he merely collected the rents…

Painting of angel playing proto-bassoon on chapel ceiling

During this period, São Cucufate continued to thrive. The walls and ceilings of the chapel were decorated with paintings of angels playing musical instruments, and a beautiful altarpiece was created by famed artisan Jose de Escovar, in the late 16th century or early 17th century.

Although no identifiable *talha* have been found in São Cucufate, we know that wine was being made in *talha* in this region in the 17th century, because a handful of *talhas* have survived nearby, signed and dated by the master craftsmen who made them. When you think of it, they were indeed masters, to create something out of terracotta that was not only utilitarian and not only beautiful, but that could last for hundreds of years.

But, by the late 17th century, Portugal's fortunes and those of the São Cucufate monastery were in decline. The buildings were eventually abandoned by the monastic community, although legend has it that one last monk refused to leave, and lived there as a hermit until his death. You can still picture him, walking through the crumbling maze of stones, climbing the old stairs to stare at the moon. Perhaps drinking the wine he had made himself, in the old way, in the terracotta pots.

After his death, the estate was occupied privately. One can imagine pleasant summer evenings listening to Renaissance and later Baroque music played under the painted ceilings, although the winter evenings, with thick cold stone walls and limited heating, were likely to have been a lot less pleasant.

The painted chapel continued to serve the small local community, hosting Sunday services, christenings, weddings and funerals.

Then, a major turning point for Portugal. In 1755, on All Saints Day, the Lisbon area was pulverized by a magnitude 9 earthquake. Gaps five meters wide opened in the center of Lisbon. The sea itself receded, beaching the ships in Lisbon's harbor, but the water returned with a vengeance, transformed into a tsunami that engulfed the city. Meanwhile, candles lit for All Saints Day had toppled, starting fires, resulting in a firestorm that burned for hours. Caught between falling stone, fire and flood, many people perished, and Lisbon itself was devastated.

The whole of southern Portugal, including Alentejo, was also hit by the quake. It is likely that São Cucufate's ancient stone walls would have been damaged, perhaps its owners killed or injured. For whatever reason, around the same time as the earthquake, São Cucufate was abandoned, and the estate progressively fell further into ruin. It seems likely that further stones were taken by local people to rebuild their homes. The pretty painted chapel became a meeting place only for pigeons.

For the next two centuries, Portugal and the Alentejo suffered through the Napoleonic wars and numerous revolutions. *Talhas* with maker's marks dating from the 1600s, 1700s, 1800s and 1900s have survived, so we can know that the *talha* tradition continued through these tumultuous times.

In 1910 the monarchy was overthrown, in 1926 there was a military coup d'etat, and in 1933 the Salazar fascist dictatorship took over. By this time, São Cucufate was in a dire state.

Finally, in 1974, the Carnation revolution overthrew the dictatorship, and a democratic government was established in 1975. The Portuguese authorities recognised the importance of this historic site and started the process of preservation, reinforcing the walls, ceilings and pavements and repairing the doors. The site was reorganized, with a formal archeological excavation established, landscaping around the periphery and the construction of an interpretative center.

And so São Cucufate is now the fascinating and well-preserved site that I saw in 2021.

Many other estates in Alentejo have followed a similar path to that of São Cucufate, albeit with less ancient foundations. Over centuries, large country properties with working farms and wine production facilities have been rebuilt, extended, renovated and upgraded. Pools have been excavated out of the spare farmyard. Large kitchens, once the heart of the working farm, have been upgraded, and rambling halls and wandering conservatories converted into function centers. Excess farm buildings have been re-roofed, re-floored, re-wired and re-plumbed to provide guest accommodation.

And like phoenixes rising from ashes, dramatic new modern wineries have arisen to replace earlier modest production facilities.

And, as they did in Roman times, every year families return from Lisbon to their vineyards to harvest their grapes and make their wine.

Much of the wine produced by these estates is sold and drunk locally, but as the quality and the reputation of Alentejo's *talha* wine increases, more and more is being produced, bottled, put onto trucks and sent off to other places, sometimes by land, sometimes by sea, where it arrives to be served at our table…and so the cycle of life goes on.

Chapter 30
Visiting the Alentejo

I am not a wine geek, although I love drinking the stuff. I am not a historian, although history enchants me. Happily, for those not totally focused on *talha* wine, there is a wealth of other aspects of the Alentejan culture to keep you more than interested; history, food, ancient sights, and of course the people.

How to get there

Luckily, the Alentejo region is very close to Portugal's capital Lisbon, one of Europe's most beautiful capital cities, served by major airlines and low-cost airlines flying routes from UK, Europe, US, Canada and South America.

If you want to fully tour *talha* territory, you need a car. Rental cars can be collected from Lisbon and Faro airports, and from sites within major towns. Portugal operates an automated toll system, so you should register for this when you collect the rental car.

If you really don't want to drive, you can get from Lisbon to Evora and/or Cuba (Beja line) by train https://www.cp.pt/passageiros/en, or buses can take you to Vidigueira, Vila Frades and Vila Alva https://www.rede-expressos.pt/.

Where to stay

As with all of Portugal, you will find a wide range of accommodation options, from luxurious and expensive, through medium-priced family and group accommodation, to inexpensive and simple, small hotels and apartments.

On the luxury end, are *Pousadas*; typically historic old castles and monasteries in special settings, converted into upmarket accommodation, and now run as part of a national chain. The pleasures of a *pousada* are that you are staying in a genuinely historic place. Prices vary depending on season, but are likely to range from 100 euros to 200 euros a night per room.

There are four *pousadas* conveniently located in the main *talha* regions of Alentejo. Staying several nights in each of these *pousadas* would be a good way to track your path through *talha* territory:

https://www.pousadas.pt/en/hotel/pousada-alvito, near Vidigueira;

https://www.pousadas.pt/en/hotel/pousada-evora, in the center of Evora;

https://www.pousadas.pt/en/hotel/pousada-estremoz, in Estremoz, and

https://www.pousadas.pt/en/hotel/pousada-marvao, north east of Portalegre.

With 'get thee to a nunnery' being somewhat common in previous ages in devout catholic Portugal, there are also a lot of convents in Alentejo, and many of these have now been converted into tourist hotels. Convents are typically more modest than *pousadas*, but no less charming. Good options include: https://www.solarmonfalim.com/, in the center of Evora; intimate, charming, wonderfully filled with historic furniture and startlingly well-priced.

Enterprising Alentejans are increasingly taking leftover bits of village buildings that they have inherited and converting them into apartments for tourists. These range from the immaculate but perhaps slightly bland, to the authentic but often less than immaculate.

Apartments in Alentejo are signed on the outside by an 'A L', and can be found via the usual suspects: Booking.com and Airbnb. You can expect to pay between 50 and 100 euros a night.

When to go

Alentejo is blessed with nearly five months of summer: mid-May through to early October. You could visit in May or June, and get good weather, blooming wild flowers, and no crowds. July and August can get hot, in the mid-30sC/90sF range. These months are the peak holiday time for Europe and so prices will be higher and accommodation may book out.

Harvest runs from late August through to early September, depending on the grape variety and the elevation of the vineyard, so you won't get quite as much attention during that period. Otherwise September-October offers pleasant weather.

The winter itself is mild, with average lows and highs ranging from 5 to 15C, often climbing into the 20s C (60s-70s F), however many of the adegas will be closed so tastings will need to be organized in advance. It is advisable to also book your accommodation in advance as this is not prime tourist territory nor prime tourist season, so accommodation options are fewer.

The very best time to go, however, is St. Martin's Day in mid-November. Then you may have the absolutely finest *talha* experience, rambling the back alleys of the *talha* villages seeking the festive opening of the *talha*, sitting at long, plain paper-decked tables, eating authentic home-made Alentejan food and drinking authentic *talha* wine with the Alentejan people.

Welcome to their world.

Chapter 31
Visiting the Regions

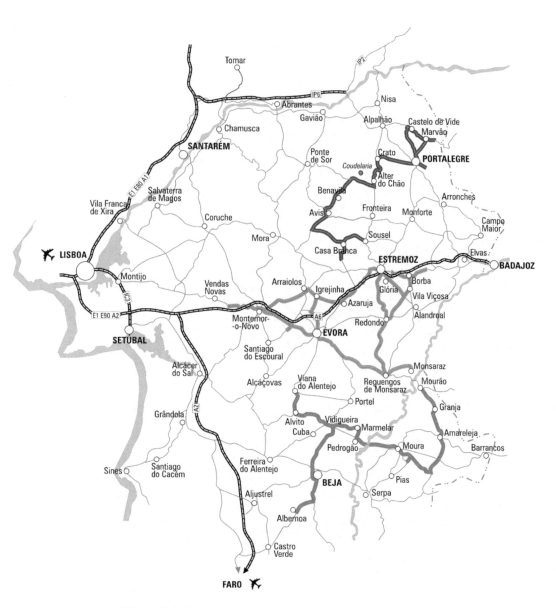

Alentejo's 3 designated wine routes. Map provided by CVRA.

Evora and Environs

Evora is a very beautiful city, full of charming streets, good shops, magnificent ruins, attractive buildings, and excellent restaurants. Visit the Saturday farmers market to buy olive oil, cheese, and *massa de pimento*. If you like it, you could also acquire a tranche of *bacalhau*.

Temple of Diana in Evora

Evocative Evora

Further out are spectacular antas and menhir: the Cromeleque dos Almendres, reputedly 3000 years older than Stonehenge, Menir dos Almendres, and the Anta Grande do Zambujeiro.

Cromeleque dos Almendres

Talha Producers

Fitapreta
Casa Relvas

Restaurants

O Fialho, Evora
Cafe Alentejo, Evora
Cartuxa, Evora

Vidigueira

The Vidigueira region is ground zero for *talha* culture. The wineries are close together so can be easily visited in the same trip. In the (possibly unlikely!) event of you having a bicycle, you could even cycle to each adega. The best time to visit is of course mid November for the St Martins Day *talha*-opening adega crawl, followed by Amphora Day at Herdade do Rocim.

Villa Aurica / Saõ Cucufate near Vidigueira; largest intact roman ruins in the Iberian peninsula (see opening chapter) is well-worth a visit, as is the Centro Interpretativo do Vinho de Talha; an excellent *talha* museum in Vila de Frades.

Talha Wine producers

ACV
Gerações da Talha
Honrado
Adega Cooperativa de Vidigueira, Cuba e Alvito
XXVI Talhas
Herdade do Rocim
Quinta da Pigarça

Restaurants

Pais das Uvas (Honrado)

For many years, António Honrado would fill several *talha* and make wine in the traditional way, and serve this wine to customers in the family's *talha taberna* Pais das Uvas in Vila de Frades.

Pais das Uvas

The Honrado family however had one major problem with serving *talha* wine in their restaurant. Their customers liked it. They liked it so much that they drank it all up by February or even earlier. And so António, son Ruben and their family decided to expand their business by investing in additional vineyards, and creating a new *talha* winemaking cellar next door (see Honrado section).

Now when the clientele come to Pais das Uvas for the food, and drink with it the wine poured from the *talha*, they will not be disappointed when the restaurant's fresh *talha* supply runs dry. The bottled range, made in *talha* but then bottled, carries on serving customers.

The food is traditional and hearty. A rank of *talha* line the whole of one wall, with several overflowing to the other side. The Honrado cellar next door is a fascinating archaeological site and well worth a visit.

Adega Canena (Quinta da Pigarça)

Further up the road, close to Cuba, the Canena family estate of Pigarça has been transitioning from general farm and equestrian business into becoming the largest producer of *talha* wine. Meanwhile, the rambling farm buildings are home to the extended Canena family: father, mother, two brothers, an uncle and aunt and cousins.

They have recently opened a *talha* adega in Cuba. Starting with a bar serving their *talha* wine and small platters of *tapiscos* - Portuguese style tapas - they will be extending into a full restaurant in 2022. *Talha* already line the walls of the new restaurant, ready and waiting to be filled, and to be emptied.

Adega Canena - getting ready for business

Monte Pedral

In the center of the village of Cuba is a sprawling white-plastered manor house; home to one of the great traditional *tabernas*: Monte Pedral, originally owned by a famous bull-fighter. At the front is an open bar, with a small *tasquinha* used to serve wine to the old men standing at the bar. Tables fill the big courtyard, and a stately row of giant *talha* mark the front of the manor house. Out the back is a room full of working *talha*, and rows of plastic carafes, showing the journey to be made by the wine; from *talha* to plastic carafe, and thence to the restaurant.

The kitchen and main dining room is housed in a single-storeyed building to one side. Inside is an odd mixture. The huge old half-stripped cork oak tree in the middle of the main dining room is made of fiberglass, (leaving the real thing to keep sucking copious quantities of CO_2 out of the environment) and the outside dining area is littered with fake Roman statues. But the food and the wine are absolutely authentic.

No English is spoken, so you will need to brush up on your Portuguese or accept whatever they decide to give you on the day. On the day we visited, we were served *pata da negra*, sliced from hams hanging over the bar, followed by *feijoada*, and slices of roast pork with fried potato, ending with honey cake, and accompanied by as much *talha* wine as we could drink, served in little carafes shaped as miniature *talha*.

The dining room at Monte Pedral

The North

A land of rolling hills leading up to steeper mountains, interspersed with rivers, vineyards, and ruins, and dotted by hill-top castles surrounded by winding cobbled streets, the northern region is one of the most beautiful parts of Alentejo.

Estremoz is a charming town, with a range of good restaurants. Nearby is where the Romans once mined marble, which may have been used for the floors of Saõ Cucufate to the south west.

You shouldn't miss a visit to the hilltop castle and village of Marvaõ.

Portalegre

Talha producers

Susana Esteban
Rui Reguinga / Terranus

Restaurants

Rio Sever Hotel Restaurant

Borba

Talha producers

Adega de Borba
Herdade dos Outeiros Altos

Restaurants

Alecrim, Estremoz

Marvaõ hilltop village

Howard's Folly, Estremoz

The South East

The area to the south east is dominated by water - the river Guadiana and the great sprawling man-made lake Lago do Alqueva. The Alentejans treat this area as their adventure park, enjoying both water sports and hunting.

Reguengos

Talha Producers

Jose de Sousa
Herdade do Esporão
Cortes de Cima

Granja-Amareleja

Talha Producers

Adega Marel

Chapter 32
Eating in Alentejo

If you drink, you must eat...

There is an old saying that 'if you drink, you must eat'. Wisely, many of the adegas that served wine direct from their *talhas* to their customers also developed a tradition of serving simple, local food to eat alongside the wine. These *talha tascas* were Alentejo's ancient vinous answer to a modern brew pub. But just as the *talha* winemaking tradition diminished over the last century, so too have the *tascas*.

Happily, with the renaissance of *talha* winemaking, there are also the early signs of the rebirth of the *talha tasca*, in the form of *tabernas*. After all, when the next generation of Alentejans look to set up a business or take on their father's, mother's or grandfather's business, isn't it really not at all surprising that they look back into their history to find - what is now the modern approach to linking food and wine? Doesn't it make obvious sense to extend their adega into a restaurant, capturing a captive market for their *talha* wine?

In some cases, the food follows the wine, as the new creators of *talha* wine expand into that wise tradition of providing accompanying food. In others, the success of a restaurant has driven the demand for more wine and an increase in *talha* winemaking. And in some, both wine and food are inextricably interdependent, feeding off each other, becoming an ecosystem that makes the whole business better.

And the food you will be offered at these *talha tabernas*? The style will be similar to those traditional *talha tabernas*, and yet a bit different. Family cooking made with fresh local produce and complex flavors, based on traditional recipes with modern twists.

An Alentejo meal will start with slices of Alentejo bread of which Alentejans are justly proud: a round, light brown, sourdough-style loaf, that is dense but light, chewy but with crisp crusts. Accompanying the bread might be Alentejo olives, perhaps a dipping bowl of spicy Alentejo olive oil, and slices of the ham from Alentejo black pigs. Other common starters are chickpeas with *bacalhau*, marinated roast peppers in olive oil and garlic, and portions of Alentejo cheese. In Alentejo, cheeses are more likely to be made from sheep or goat milk than cow's milk, and will be pale yellow, ripened, hard or semi-hard shaped in small, circular rounds, served with walnuts and dried apricots, or slices of fresh apple or quince.

Alentejans, like many Portuguese, often eat their daily dose of vegetables as a soup before the main course. Three of the most famous vegetarian Alentejo soups are: *acorda*, made from broth, bread, coriander and poached egg, *sopa de tomate à Alentejana*, a creamy tomato soup often topped with shoestring fried potatoes, and *gazpacho Alentejana*, in which the vegetables are served in chunks not pureed. This gazpacho is said to have been the hot summer's day meal for workers in the field; freshly chopped vegetables just needing the addition of refreshing ice-cold water.

Feijoada is a famous Brazilian and Portuguese soup stew, consisting in a broth with either white beans or chickpeas, pork, ham, sausage, plus added vegetables such as onion, tomato, carrots. This is a hearty soup for winter, so hearty that *feijoada* can act as your main meal.

Main course specialties of Alentejo include: in spring: *porco Alentejana* - pork and clams, or roast leg of suckling lamb (you are served a whole small leg, best not to picture the baby lamb it came from), in summer: barbecued skewers of fish, seafood and peppers or lamb chunks with peppers. In autumn, game, especially wild boar or venison, or duck legs, cooked with Portuguese chorizo and rice. In winter: lamb stew, or pork roasted in red pepper paste, or chicken cooked with rice.

And in all seasons, of course, fish. (Paul: Which do you recommend, the venison or the partridge? Waiter: 'I prefer the fish'...)

A simple meal at a village *taberna*

Alentejans love their fish, which can seem surprising because Alentejo is mostly inland. But the Portuguese have always been a sea-faring people, and their hearts and stomachs seem to long for fish, and salted fish at that. Cod, being both plentiful and easy to preserve in salt, became the chosen fish for *bacalhau* - without question the most favored Portuguese food.

Bacalhau is the one major Portuguese food that comes from far away; originally Newfoundland (several centuries before Columbus set sail) but now most often Norway. The Portuguese eat around a million kilos of *bacalhau* every year. According to popular myth, there are 365 different ways to cook *bacalhau*. It can be baked, fried, grilled, poached, as a starter, in a soup, as a main dish - you name it. I have not yet been served *bacalhau* for dessert, which I consider a mercy.

Main courses are likely to be accompanied by boiled new potatoes, or fried regular potatoes, or rice, or *migas*, made of leftover bread, soaked then flavored and fried. The Alentejo version of *migas* is made with finely chopped black olives and thistle.

Salads might be either plain lettuce with sliced tomato and cucumber, or slightly more upmarket: Alentejo watercress with fresh coriander.

Deserts are typically made of egg, egg and egg, and, like *bacalhau*, also prepared in 365 different ways, although my favourite traditional Alentejo recipe is *bolo de mel Alentejana*; walnut and honey cake.

Chapter 33
For the Virtual Tourist

If you are a long way from the Alentejo, you might like to prepare the following:

Bread soup with coriander and egg

Acorda - Bread soup with Coriander

Ingredients for 6 servings

A large bunch of fresh coriander
2 garlic cloves
4 Tbsp olive oil
1 Tbsp salt
6 eggs
3-4 slices of sourdough bread, torn into rough chunks, optionally fried in olive oil

Preparation

Make a pesto with the coriander, garlic, olive oil and salt (using a mortar and pestle, or blender).

Spoon the pesto into the bottom of 6 soup bowls.

Poach the eggs in 1-2 liters boiling water until the whites are firm but the yolk is still runny; about 3 minutes.

Add the chunks of bread to each bowl.

Add about a cup of the boiling water from the poached eggs.

Top each serving with a poached egg

Variations

You can add a portion of reconstituted *bacalhau* to the soup prior to adding the bread and egg.

Include poached fish as well as or instead of the egg.

Serve with a white *talha* wine.

Porco Alentejana

Pork with clams, Alentejan style

Ingredients for 6 servings

1kg good quality pork filet, cut into chunks

2 tbsp red pepper paste

1 tsp hot paprika

2-3 garlic cloves, crushed

300ml dry white wine

olive oil

1 onion, chopped

800g raw clams, scrubbed

handful coriander, chopped

salt and freshly ground black pepper

Potatoes

Preparation

Put the pork chunks in a bowl. Add the red pepper paste, paprika, garlic and wine.

Cover, transfer to the fridge and marinate for a few hours or overnight.

Dice the potatoes, toss in olive oil and place in a preheated oven.

Strain the pork and reserve the marinade.

Heat 2–3 tablespoons of oil in a large heavy-bottomed pot. Brown the pork in batches. Reserve.

Add 2tbsps olive oil and fry the onion. When the onion is soft, return all the pork to the pan, stir in the reserved marinade. Turn up the heat and bring to the boil. Continue to cook until the liquid is reduced by half.

When the potatoes are done:

Discard any clams which stay open after you tap them. Add the clams to the pot, cover and cook until the clams have steamed open (3-5 minutes). Discard any clams that do not open after cooking.

Toss, season with salt and pepper, scatter the coriander over and serve with the roasted potatoes, to soak up the juice.

Variations

If you don't have red pepper paste, blitz some preserved red peppers with olive oil and add salt.

Serve with a red *talha* wine.

Bolo de Mel Alentejana - Honey cake

This cake keeps very well, so can be made in advance and stored in an airtight container.

It is often eaten at Christmas.

Ingredients

200ml olive oil

200ml of Alentejo honey

4 eggs, separated

125g brown sugar

zest of 1 lemon or half an orange

250g wholemeal flour

1 teaspoon of baking powder

1 teaspoon of cinnamon

1/2 teaspoon powdered cloves

50-100g walnuts, chopped

Extra walnuts and/or blanched almonds for decoration.

Preparation

Line a cake tin bottom with baking paper. You can use either a large or a small cake tin. The resulting cake will be corresponding low or high.

Lightly grease the paper and the sides.

Beat the oil with the honey until it thickens.

Add the yolks one by one, beating well, then the orange or lemon zest and half the sugar.

Separately, sift the flour with the baking powder, cinnamon and cloves.

Beat the whites until soft peaks form.

Gradually add the rest of the sugar, sifted to remove lumps.

Fold in one third of the egg white mixture to the oil and honey mixture.

Add half the flour mixture, mixing gently. Add another third of the egg whites.

Add the rest of the flour and the walnuts. Add the last third of the egg whites.

Pour the mixture into cake tin, press extra walnuts (and/or almonds) onto surface

Bake in a medium oven (180ºC) for 35-40 minutes.

When cool, turn out. Sprinkle lightly with icing sugar.

Variation

Instead of walnuts, use almonds.

Place these on the surface of the cake before putting the cake in the oven.

Serve with more *talha* wine, either (or both) red and white

Lay your table with a Portuguese linen tablecloth.

Put on some *Cante Alentejo* music.

And enjoy…

Biographies

Expat-American Paul White divides his time between Languedoc, London, Oregon and New Zealand. Paul began exploring wine during Oregon's pioneering days in the 1970s. Shifting gears in the 1980s, he relocated to Europe to undertake a Doctorate in Music at Oxford University. While captaining the University's Blind Wine-tasting team, he began a more serious study of Europe's classic wine regions and emerging wine cultures around the world.

Carrying on from that experience, he turned his attention to Australasian wine, working as a wine journalist based in New Zealand during the 1990s and 2000s.

Paul White, proud father

More recently, the family purchased the gatehouse of an old Cathar castle near Carcassonne in France, and since then he's refocused attention back onto European wine. After a spell writing for Slow Food Italy and World of Fine Wine, he developed a special interest in preserving family-sized wine producers, endangered grapes, traditional viticulture and terracotta winemaking. Paul has a longstanding empathy for outsiders, underdogs and lost causes.

He has managed to visit 90 wine regions in over twenty countries on six continents, while also judging 60+ international wine competitions.

You can follow more of Paul's wine adventures on www.winedisclosures.com.

Jennifer Mortimer started her working life as a computer programmer but has since broadened her horizons into general management and project management. She has recently branched out into writing, managing Visual Effects R&D for the film industry, and X-Reality production. She is currently managing the delivery of an ecological Immersive Learning project based on Virtual Reality technology.

Herding Paul into completing this book has, however, been her most challenging project to date.

Jennifer Mortimer at the Amphora Day launch of Talha Tales

Bibliographic References

Talha, *Qvevri*, *Karas* and Amphora links

https://www.winedisclosures.com/amphora-triptych/alentejos-talha-tradition
https://www.winedisclosures.com/amphora-triptych/qvevri-georgias-amphora
https://www.winedisclosures.com/amphora-triptych/karas-amphora-in-armenia

Chapter 2

Check out Alentejo CVR's delightful video synopsis of the *talha* winemaking process
https://www.youtube.com/watch?v=ZzVGkmY41BI

Chapter 7

https://www.winedisclosures.com/endangered-grapes
https://www.vinetowinecircle.com/genetica/reflexoes-acerca-da-presenca-de-vitis-silvestris-na-iberia-urante-a-era-glaciar/
https://www.vinetowinecircle.com/historia/idade-bronze-iber/
https://www.vinetowinecircle.com/en/history/the-time-of-the-roman-empire/
López-Ruiz and Pérez, S. C., 2016. *Tartessos and the Phoenicians in Iberia*; Oxford University Press, p192-193.
A. Lavrador da Silva, M. João Fernão-Pires F. Bianchi-de-Aguiar, 2018. *Portuguese vines and wines: heritage, quality symbol, tourism asset a vinha* ; printed in Ciência Téc. Vitiv. 33(1). p31-46.

Chapter 8

Peña, J.T. 2007. *Roman Pottery in the Archaeological Record*; Cambridge University Press
McGovern, P. 2019. *Ancient Wine: The Search for the Origins of Viniculture*; Princeton University Press
López-Ruiz, C. 2021. *Phoenicians and the Making of the Mediterranea*; Harvard University Press
Pérez, S.C., and López-Ruiz, C. 2016. *Tartessos and the Phoenicians in Iberia*; Oxford University Press
Dias Viegas, C., P. A. Carretero, M.D. Petit Dominguez, M.I. Rucandio, R. Vigil de la Villa and R. Garcia Gimenez. *Characterization of Dolia from the Guadalquivir Valley and found in the Southern Lusitania Sites (Algarve, Portugal)*

Glossary of Terms

Adega Common Portuguese term for winery.

Bâtonnage A process where the settled dead-yeast lees is stirred back into the clear young wine sitting above, with the intention of increasing texture and amplifying aromas. A *talha's* natural internal convection currents do this automatically rather than with the traditional use of a baton.

Clone A genetic variation of a specific grape variety, derived through mutation that produces slightly different characteristics. High clonal variation suggests longevity in a specific place.

Herdade Common Portuguese term for farm or homestead, mostly used in Alentejo.

Lagar A stone-walled tank used for treading grapes with the feet.

Mae The 'mother', consisting of pulp, dead-yeast lees, skins and stems contained within the *talha's* belly.

Palhete A traditional local everyday wine style made from a mixture of white and red grapes, fermented together, resulting in a wine that is somewhere between rose and a light red.

Pés A melted concoction of beeswax, pine sap, olive oil and various herbs applied to the inside of a *talha* to prevent seepage and regulate oxygen transference.

Petiscos Small plates of finger food similar to Spanish tapas.

Quinta Common Portuguese term for vineyard or grapevine-focused farm.

Qvevri Georgia's ancient buried form of winemaking pot going back 6000-8000 years. Similar in size and shape to *talha*, qvevri (from the word *kveuri* meaning something buried) lack a lower drainage hole and maintain longer skin contact with wine, resulting in more tannic 'orange' wine styles.

Skin Contact Extended maceration process combining grape pulp and skins, producing increased tannins.

Taberna A combination of a largish *talha* winery and a restaurant.

Talha A Portuguese form of terracotta winemaking pot with a low positioned drainage hole, that has been in continuous use at least since the Roman era. Pronounced somewhere between tal-ha and tal-yah

Tasca A smaller, cafe-sized *taberna* serving *petiscos*.

Tareco or *Tarefa* A smaller-sized *talha* that supplies family needs through to the next vintage.

The End

We hope you have enjoyed the journey through *talha* territory. We will be updating these pages in the future, as more *talha* wines are made, and as more secrets emerge.

To stay informed, please visit https://www.winedisclosures.com/.

Talhas in the wild…

Printed in Great Britain
by Amazon